SNAKES
& LIZARDS

SNAKES & LIZARDS

•TOM LANGTON•

with illustrations by
DENYS OVENDEN

Whittet Books

Endpaper: *adder and common lizard.*

First published 1989
Text © 1989 by Tom Langton
Illustrations © 1989 by Denys Ovenden
Whittet Books Ltd, 18 Anley Road, London W14 0BY

British Library Cataloguing in Publication Data
Langton, Tom
    Snakes and lizards
    1. Lizards 2. Snakes
    I. Title
    597.95

ISBN 0-905483-77-4

Typeset by Camelot Typesetters, Bristol BS12 6UX
Printed and bound by Biddles of Guildford

Contents

Acknowledgments

There are several people quietly working to study and protect snakes and lizards whom I have been lucky enough to work with, accompany in the field and learn from. Several made useful comments and corrections to the draft manuscript. Some have worked with tireless energy to battle against the losses of reptile habitats, and to carry out reptile habitat restoration. Others have raised grants or otherwise supported reptile conservation projects in which I have been involved over the last twelve years, including members and staff from the Nature Conservancy Council, the World Wide Fund for Nature, the Fauna and Flora Preservation Society, County Museums, County Conservation Trusts, and officers of County and District Local Authorities, H.M. Customs and Excise and Departments of Environment and Transport Societas Europaea Herpetologica and the Vincent Wildlife Trust. These include Henry Arnold, Roger Avery, Brian Banks, Catherine Beckett, Antony Braithwaite, Trevor Beebee, John Buckley, John Burton, Bruce Coleman, Arnold Cooke, Keith Corbett, the Earl of Cranbrook, David and Marion Dalton, Colin Fitzsimmons, John Goldsmith, Howard Inns, Mark Jones, Gabriel King, Ian Prestt, Mike Preston, David Race, Bob Stebbings, David Stubbs, Ian Swingland, Jonathan Taylor, Chris Tydeman, Malcolm Vincent, Edward Wade, Jonathan Webster, Derek Whitely and Bill Whittaker. Those who have helped herpetofauna conservation from the world of business and industry include Derek Humphries, Robin Lipscombe, John Osbourne, Richard Stevens, Stephen Rubin and Edward Wright. Thanks are also due to writers and broadcasters who have helped to project a positive image of reptiles to the public and to all those who I have not remembered to list who have helped with the understanding and conservation of reptiles.

Preface

The fear of snakes (ophidophobia) will prevent some people from reading, looking at or even touching this book. In most people, this fear is based on lack of knowledge and misunderstanding rather than any real threat. Snakes and lizards are used symbolically; in Europe, the most widespread image of snakes has been the religious representation of the serpent as sin and the devil. Snakes have unfortunately become the faults of humankind personified. On the television or cinema screens, the gasp-and-laugh scariness of snake-pits or cartoon lizard-monsters thrill, because we can laugh at what at other times may frighten.

One of the most frequent reactions to snakes is, 'I just don't like them.' This often seems to be justified by an assumption that such an attitude is natural. We are trying to dispel unfounded prejudices towards unpopular species, such as British spiders, which would be hard pushed to tickle you to death, or bats, unjustifiably blamed for tangling in people's hair; snakes and lizards too need friends who will protect them from persecution and prevent their numbers from declining further.

Most people in Britain have never had more than a fleeting glimpse of a wild snake or lizard, and so attitudes towards them are moulded by hearsay and imagery. There are many places around the world where reptiles come into contact with humans; in Africa, Asia and tropical America thousands of people are laid up in hospital or are killed outright from venomous snake bites every year. We in Britain have lost our 'dangerous' animals — our wolves and bears — so it is easy to accept unquestioningly established views and reactions. People kill snakes not only because they fear being bitten but because of a conditioned response: a practical demonstration of the ability to conquer evil. The killing of snakes is really another form of ritual killing.

In general, snakes have never recovered from the bad press they got in the Garden of Eden (see 'Thou art cursed'). In recent years, public awareness campaigns to 'Be kind to snakes' have attempted to change the image of reptiles, and popular interest is growing. Perhaps one day reptiles will receive the same popular following as birds with their admiring following armed with back garden food, bird tables and binoculars. A star rating for reptiles would promote rockeries for lizards and frog ponds for grass snakes.

In the animal ratings, fur, big eyes and round faces are preferred to bald, scuttling, thin-legged skulkers. Before we lose our wild inhabitants, whether they are conventionally beautiful or not (which is anyway a matter of taste), let us hope we recognize their value.

This book mainly concerns reptiles found in Britain, but refers to Europe, where all these species also live. I have written this book in the hope that it will interest those already converted to the maintenance of our natural heritage, and inform those who may be 'dipping in' to the subject for the first time. I hope that it will provide an insight into the lives of reptiles, and convince readers, who will convert others by word of mouth, that snakes and lizards need our support.

Tom Langton
Walpole, Suffolk 1989

Who's who?

The saying that bad things often come in threes must, thankfully, exclude snakes and lizards, for there are three kinds of snake and three kinds of lizard in Britain. One type of lizard, the slow-worm, is legless and at first sight looks quite snake-like. Reptiles can be difficult to identify, but with a little practice, as with bird-watching, they can often be distinguished from a fleeting glance.

All six British reptile species have large European ranges. Common lizards and adders are found as far away as the Pacific coast of Russia, some are found within the Arctic circle. Grass snakes are found as far south as the north African countries of Morocco and Algeria and Tunisia. Numbers of reptiles in Britain's populations represent only a tiny percentage of the total numbers of these species in the world, but this should not undermine their importance. It shows that we have reptiles which are adaptable, and widespread. This gives even more reason for concern about their decline in Britain. They are not delicate indicator species, but animals which are being lost from Britain as a result of human population expansion, which is causing destruction and pollution of their environment.

Scales and tails

The most widespread snake is the northern viper, commonly referred to as the adder. Adults rarely exceed 66 cm (26 inches) in Britain, though older records exist of adders approaching lengths of 91 cm (36 inches). Colours of adders vary, and, as with all reptiles, may become dull as sloughing (skin shedding) approaches. The background coloration of male adders is usually a light shade of grey or brown with a well defined black zig-zag marking along the length of the back. Females have a darker background colour with browner zig-zag markings. A V-shaped marking at the back of the head usually precedes the zig-zag. The underside of adders can be shades of grey, brown or black, sometimes with white spots and faint tinges of other colours. The iris of the eye is a shade of red with a black vertical pupil.

The grass snake reaches the largest size of any British snake, and is found in Wales and England but rarely Scotland. Even in England, grass snakes

British snakes: 1/1a. grass snake 2/2a. adder 3/3a. smooth snake.

become very scarce as you travel north beyond the Midlands. Adult female grass snakes approaching 178 cm (70 inches) in length have been recorded; like adders, grass snakes seem to have been recorded in greater sizes in the last century. Today males in Britain seldom exceed 90 cm (35 inches), though huge grass snakes in excess of 2 metres (78 inches) have been reported from elsewhere in the world. Adult females average about 75 cm (30 inches) in length and males 60 cm (23½ inches). Grass snakes can usually be sexed by counting the scales on the underside of the tail, which are arranged like a spread-out hand of playing cards. Between the vent and tail-tip, more than 62 scales almost always indicates a male, and less than 62 indicates a female. Typically females have 56 scales and males 66. Maximum counts of tail scales may reach 72. Scale counting is not an easy task at the best of times and on hot sunny days, an energetic snake can make it a very tricky pastime! The basic background colour of grass snakes is a shade of dark green. The body is marked with black vertical bars and spots which run along the sides. A characteristic collar in a shade between whitish yellow and orange-red is usually present, in front of a less even and incomplete black collar which may extend a little way down the side of the body. The occasional presence of light-coloured body stripes could indicate the snake is a released pet. These may even cross breed with local stock. Such animals were imported until recently in their thousands; many are known to have escaped or been released into the wild.

Smooth snakes are today confined mainly to Dorset, parts of south-west Hampshire and a handful of sites elsewhere in southern England. They rarely exceed 70 cm (27½ inches) in length in the UK, although I can personally vouch for an individual of 72 cm (28 inches) total length. Smooth snakes have round pupils to their eyes. Sexes are often difficult to determine without careful examination in the hand to measure tail and body length, and you can count tail scales. Smooth snakes normally have a grey or grey-brown background colouration with usually two rows of darker brown or black markings along the back. The rows start from the edge of an inverted, heart-shaped marking beginning on the scales on the top of the head. Underneath, I have observed shades of yellow, orange, purple and black coloration. There is a dark, roughly horizontal stripe either side of the eye.

Slow-worms are found throughout mainland Britain, and have an almost cylindrical body which is hard and smooth to the touch. Adult males are smaller than females, which may reach a length of 54 cm (21 inches). The tail (below the vent) may be a little longer than the body, and in males, as with snakes, is longer and larger at the base.

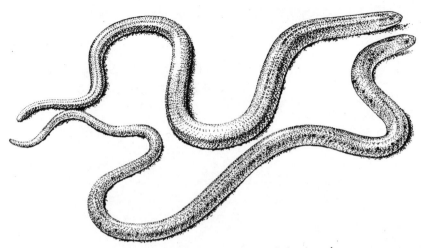

Slow-worms: (above) *female;* (below) *male.*

At birth, slow-worms are shades of coppery gold with vivid dark brown sides. A single dark spot is often found at the back of the top of the head, and from this a very fine dark line runs along the back. The striped appearance gradually fades with age but is almost always retained in females. Males often darken to shades of grey and brown, occasionally with a few blue spots which can be quite iridescent. Slow-worms have a polished appearance. The underside is usually black. Slow-worms, unlike snakes, have movable eyelids.

Like the smooth snake, the sand lizard's fragmented range now restricts it to a few areas in southern Britain. It is also found in small numbers on what remains of the Sefton sand dune system on the Merseyside coast, where it has declined and it is only just surviving. In Britain sand lizards may attain a size of about 20 cm (8 inches) from head to tail. Generally speaking, these lizards have a grey-beige background colour, covered with irregular shaped rows of dark brown blotches, which can give the appearance of three long brown stripes down the back and flanks. The blotches sometimes contain small single light brown dots. Populations may differ, some with more spotty or stripy forms. The underside is usually a shade of pale white, yellow or green. Males have thicker bases to their tail, and have greener flanks which become quite vivid during the breeding season.

In hatchlings, rows of light spots with dark borders are very noticeable and these develop to form part of the adult body pattern.

(Top pair) *Sand Lizards:* (above)*male;* (below) *female.*
(Pair below) *Viviparous or common lizard:* (above) *male;* (below) *female.*

The common lizard, otherwise called the viviparous lizard, occurs throughout Britain, and is the only reptile that has colonized Ireland. Adults usually attain a maximum size of 14 cm (5½ inches), although one individual of 17.8 cm (7 inches) has been recorded. As juveniles they are tiny, and usually dark in colour, sometimes almost black. As they mature, colour variation includes shades of brown, grey and dark green. Males retain an even colouration with light, usually pale brown flecks along the back and flanks. In females these are more substantial and may join up to give a broader striped appearance, but it can be difficult to distinguish sexes by colour. The belly may be shades of white, yellow, orange or red and is more likely to have dark spots in male lizards.

Marine turtles are now formally considered part of the British reptile fauna, one species, the leathery turtle, occurring as a regular migrant. They are occassionally reported as offshore sightings, coastline strandings or when snarled in the nets or lines of fishing trawlers (see 'Turtle diary').

Names, ancient and modern

The earliest words for reptiles usually lump them with small 'creatures' into a glorious category of 'creeping or crawling things'. The word 'lizard' seems to have the simplest derivation, from the French name *'lézard'* and the Latin *'Lacerta'* for the same animal.

On a local and regional basis, and with changing languages, the identification and naming of reptiles often varies. Shakespeare described snakes as 'worms', and, as with many animals, there has been some confusion from old records due to the use of local nicknames. These are sometimes still in use in remoter parts. The German word for snake *'nadder'* is the probable origin of our word 'adder'. The name adder has also been reported as emerging from the old Anglo-Saxon word *'naedre'*, meaning 'creeping thing'. The Latin scientific name for the adder *Vipera berus,* uses another general word for a snake, *'berus',* generally thought to mean 'live-bearing snake'. Until quite recently adders were referred to as 'hag-worms' by some local communities. The grass snake's Latin name *Natrix natrix* is derived from *'nato',* 'I swim'. The German word for grass snake is *'ringelnadder'* or 'ringed snake', referring to its bright collar. In Britain, the grass snake has also been referred to as the green, common, water or hedge snake. The smooth snake is so called because of its smooth unridged scales, while its Latin name *Coronella austriaca* refers to its head and neck markings (*'corona'* means 'crown'), and also to its distribution (*'austriaca'* means 'of the south').

The English name sand lizard (*Lacerta agilis*) comes from its favourite British terrain.

Lacerta vivipara, the viviparous lizard, comes from the joining of the Latin words *'vivus',* 'alive', and *pareo,* 'I bring forth'.

Slow-worms are, despite their name, quite fast when surprised, though if watched undisturbed they move about in a slowish fashion. However I am not convinced by this explanation of the common or vernacular name. The scientific name *Anguis fragilis* means snakelike and fragile. They are reported to have been commonly called deaf-adders in the early 1900s in the Warlingham/Chesham area, and have nicknames in other parts of Britain such as 'blindworm'.

Class distinction

Order	Sub order		Approximate number of species
Squamata	Sauria	(lizards)	3,750
	Ophidia (Serpentes)	(snakes)	2,550
	Amphisbaenia	(worm lizards)	140
Chelonia		(freshwater turtles, (terrapins), sea turtles and tortoises)	250
Rhynochocephalia		(tuatara)	1
Crocodylia		(alligators, crocodiles and gharials)	22

The class *Reptilia*, or reptiles, consists of a diverse group of animals which includes sea turtles, tortoises and crocodilians as well as snakes and lizards. All these animals differ from mammals and birds in that their body temperature is not raised substantially by their own internal 'burning of food' (metabolism), but by that of their surrounding environment. There are other differences: snakes and lizards have teeth which are continually replaced throughout life, and there are other characteristic differences in their skeletons and internal and external functioning and appearance. The

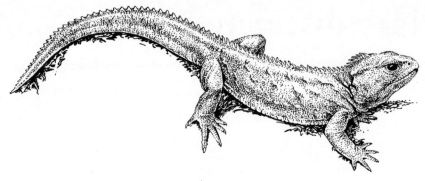

A tuatara.

class *Reptilia* also includes Amphisbaenians or worm lizards, and a single ancient lizard-like reptile known as the tuatara. The latter, incredibly, are the remaining members of a lizard-like group of animals which roamed Europe and much of the world even before the dinosaurs appeared. They inhabit about thirty small islands off the coast of New Zealand, and may live to be over one hundred years old.

Snakes and lizards of the order *Squamata* take their name from the Latin word *'squames'* which refers to the flat toughened skin or scales that are characteristic of snakes and lizards. This comprises two sub-orders *Sauria* and *Ophidia* which have developed alongside each other over millions of years. There are over 3,750 types of lizard. About 2,400-2,700 kind of snake have been described as distinct species. New species are found every year and arguments about when a variation within a species justifies a separate name mean that it will be a long time before we will actually decide on a fixed number. Snake species are divided up into over 418 genera and 11 families according to their patterns of taxonomic relationship.

Over 80 per cent of the species of snakes in the world are harmless to man, and most, like the grass snake and smooth snake, belong to the *Colubridae* family, though some of these may have small, venomous rear-fangs. Snakes can be found around the world except in most Arctic and Antarctic regions, New Zealand and a number of offshore islands. There are several families of little known snakes such as blind snakes and shieldtail snakes, and some species are very secretive. The boas and pythons are perhaps the best known families with about 67 species around the world. Both are widespread across the earth, yet they do not overlap much in distribution on each continent. Venomous snakes include over 180 species in the *Viperidae* family, which encompasses the adder and other European vipers.

Biggest snake

Fossil records indicate that the ancient boas may have been only slightly bigger than the largest snakes found on earth today. There is however some controversy as to which snake holds the record today: one problem is that snakes can naturally stretch and contract. Another is that it takes a lot of courageous, strong people to manhandle a tape measure along a powerful snake which has a huge mouth and long sharp teeth. The longest snake species are the reticulated python and the anaconda, both of which reach lengths of between 9 and 10 metres (27 and 30 feet). No one has claimed the $5,000 reward offered by the New York Zoological Society for a substantiated record of an anaconda of at least 10 metres (30 feet). One unsubstantiated record length of about 11.4 metres (34 feet) belongs to an anaconda from Colombia. Three other species — the African python, Indian python and Amethystine python — may regularly reach lengths of 6 metres (20 feet) or more, while there are a dozen or so species which may attain lengths in the 3 to 6 metre (10—19 foot) range; the rest of the 2,700 or so species do not exceed lengths of about 3 metres (10 feet).

Sea, sun and sand

Sea

Fossil and pollen records show that our climate has varied greatly in the past. Some of the reptiles today found only in warmer European climates were, until relatively recently, roaming the British countryside. Reptiles, including those seen today, will have inhabited Britain between Ice Ages prior to the last one.

About 10,000 years ago, just after the last ice age, Britain would have been a cold place unsuitable for our present-day reptiles. As the ice melted and sea levels rose to fill, what we now call the English Channel, Ireland and then mainland Britain gradually became separated from the rest of Europe. Temperatures increased, and reptiles moved northward from the warmer parts of Europe into Britain using a land bridge which is thought to have been submerged about 8,700 years ago. During this time reptiles had an additional benefit because grassland and heathland (which they prefer) were predominant; it was some time before trees dominated the British landscape.

Post-glacial human hunter gatherers and other mammals would have been

living in these areas already. Gradually as conditions became suitable, high forest developed, which was less suitable for reptiles; however, settlement clearings e.g. places where charcoal was made, the effects of animal grazing, and fires, combined with extensive undisturbed sand dunes, open flood plains, river and coastlines would all have provided exposed semi-natural or natural conditions for reptiles to flourish. As temperatures increased, the colonization of reptiles could well have been speeded by human spread, both deliberate and accidental.

Sun

Once woodland had become established, with trees like oak, elm, alder, hazel and pine competing for the warmth of the sun, reptile distribution must have declined. The maximum cover of woodland was about 7,000 years ago, some considerable time after the reptiles recolonized Britain. During this 'optimum temperature' period, air temperatures were 1°-2° higher than now.

Despite early human settlement opening woodland across much of the land, reptile distribution must then have contracted. Following climatic fluctuations — often with much cooler temperatures — Britain may then have lost some of the species now found in continental Europe — the European pond terrapin and possibly the green lizard, for example.

Mesolithic and then Neolithic civilizations cleared trees, extending

heathlands and leaving earthworks such as the Bronze Age barrows and burial mounds (tumuli) now so frequently favoured by snakes and lizards. Many lowland areas such as East Anglia then saw extensive flooding during Roman times and we should realize that since the ice age there have been extensive natural upheavals in the landscape that have channelled and squeezed reptiles into the distributions we see today. Further fossil finds may help our understanding of the exact processes of reptile colonization.

Sand

During the period of reptile invasion, when the countryside was undergoing many changes, what were the open places that reptiles used? Many must have flourished on poor soils suitable for open, patchy tree growth. These by coincidence may in some cases have been good places for human habitation. Sandy soils for example have many uses: they drain well and are good for excavation. Clear spring water sometimes emerges to form clean natural ponds at the joining of sand and other strata. Human habitations may have been sited in open areas to avoid stealthy approach from enemies and also to provide a safer way to keep watch on livestock.

Open areas were often created by fires. Fire must have occasionally devastated huge areas of scrub and open heathland. Other influences opening up heathlands included heather turf-cutting (turbary). This was carried out for a number of uses, including for fuel, forage for cattle, pigs and horses. Turf was also cut for roofing material. The effects of domestic animal grazing would have extended and maintained the natural coastal and inland heaths creating vast tracts, still excellent strongholds for reptiles today.

Most of the British reptiles have patterns and coloration which resemble the vegetation that they inhabit. Some, like the sand lizard, which normally lay their eggs in open sand, require particular soil types.

Habitats

When snakes and lizards are found in areas with richer soil it is often on silty wetlands where open conditions are created by periodic flooding, where most types of tree do not flourish. Reptiles need dry ground to overwinter, so places where poor soils like sand and gravel border with wetlands often provide suitable conditions. Where flooding regularly occurs and trees may find existence difficult due to waterlogging, reptiles may have few safe places to overwinter and so they may seek higher ground. The English Fens — the flat area south and west of the Wash — is a good example of this, as there are few records of reptiles here. Wetland areas may become overgrown. Reptiles need to seek out the warmest places to rest, feed, digest, sunbathe and otherwise recharge their batteries. This means that reptiles may require considerable movements or migrations which may be seasonal or more frequent. Grass snakes, for example, might move over a mile from a hot sunny hedgerow, down into a ditch system beside a river pasture. There they might swim, drink and feed perhaps on toads for a few months prior to returning to the very same hedgerow to overwinter again. Reptiles may use several types of habitat according to their needs and may move even more than a mile depending on the constraints of the available habitat.

Reptiles thrive in a variety of conditions determined by the availability of food, sunlight and refuges. Common lizards, for example, might typically be found on grassy embankments, but may be just as successful living by a cold Scottish loch-side shrouded in mist, only emerging during a few hot sunny periods each summer month to bask and feed on flies on the edge of a sea-sprayed rock. On the Continent, warmer conditions allow greater freedom of movement and the use of a wider variety of habitats.

Dry heathlands are the best recognized habitat for reptiles in Britain. They consist of characteristic combinations of young trees, shrubs and grasses. Heather heathland (*Callunetum*) is dominated by ling (*Calluna vulgaris*). This purple flowered landscape can reach a great age with some plants being as old as the trees on adjacent woodland; others will have died or been stunted by heather beetle attack, frost, fires, grazing, wild animal activity, erosion and human influences, creating a mosaic pattern of plants of many ages.

Areas which may become open because of one or more of the above factors can be important to reptiles. At one place in the Netherlands for example dozens of sand lizard eggs have been found close together in small patches of open sand eroded by the elements or bared by wild animals. The sand lizard benefits from areas of firm, warm, open sand where a short tunnel can be dug and the eggs left to hatch. Sand lizards are sometimes associated with disturbed or 'boundary' habitats on reclaimed heathland where the soil surface is in some way disrupted, perhaps by a track or bridleway. This creates conditions where sand lizards and other reptiles can exploit resources not previously available to them, so population densities can be very high.

Semi-natural habitats that are similar to natural heathland include railway embankments, forest rides, sea walls, quarry and reservoir banks, road verges, golf courses, airfields, car park borders, escarpments, ruins, burial mounds, churchyards and certain types of garden. In fact almost any area

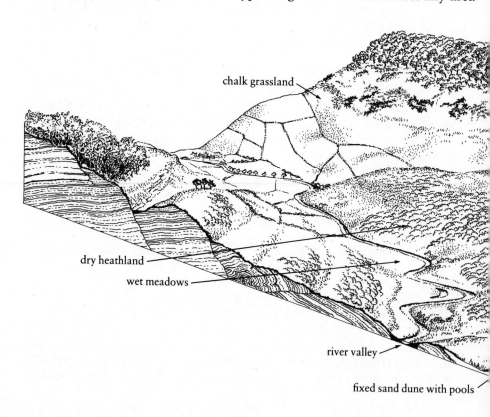

chalk grassland

dry heathland

wet meadows

river valley

fixed sand dune with pools

with a sunny, south facing slope and open vegetation may be suitable for reptiles. On dune systems, the more mature dune slopes with older dying-back marram, bramble and creeping willow are often favoured, but the wilder, wind-blown frontal dunes with marram and red fescue grasses may also hold good numbers. Reptiles may thrive in grassland, on chalk, limestone, coal and other strata.

The network of railway embankments in Britain, despite their occasional soaking with chemical sprays or burning of vegetation, can provide good lizard habitats; churchyard grassland between gravestones may be homes to reptiles, particularly grass snakes and slow-worms. The retention of heat by stone makes for good basking and sheltering spots. It has even been suggested that the south-east facing slopes and walls of upland farms are

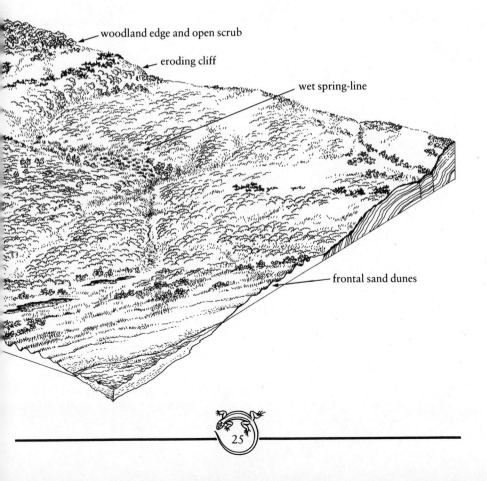

woodland edge and open scrub

eroding cliff

wet spring-line

frontal sand dunes

vital in enabling common lizards to survive there. Snakes and lizards may bask on ant hills and use the tunnel systems of small mammals as retreats.

The need to heat up means that reptiles are attracted to materials that absorb and retain heat: glass, metal, wood, paper, plastic and other debris, which may be scattered on unmanaged land, often provides the advantage of warm shelter. Even in some of the hottest areas of Europe reptiles can be observed in warm, sheltered spots. In northern Greece I recently found a nose-horned viper curled neatly beneath a discarded rusting shovel. For

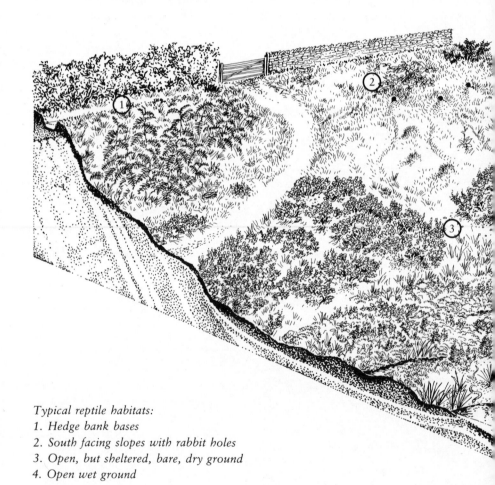

Typical reptile habitats:
1. *Hedge bank bases*
2. *South facing slopes with rabbit holes*
3. *Open, but sheltered, bare, dry ground*
4. *Open wet ground*

just a few hours before the sun was high in the sky, the early-morning rays had been concentrated on the metal and the snake was taking advantage of them to warm away the chill of night. A warmer, longer day may assist a snake's digestion, incubation of young and reduce the risks of exposed basking. Reptiles are often attracted into wastelands and rubbish tips, though the benefits of such places can be short-lived.

More stable natural conditions for reptiles do, however, occur: glacial channels, for example, which are the wide ditches eroded away in the ground

by melting glacial ice. Such channels used to carry melt water across the north-east Yorkshire moors, but are now dry; tiny, steep-sided valleys winding through the landscape, they are filled with bushy heather, grasses and lichens and have thriving populations of lizards. Other suitable habitats include ancient and modern excavations from human settlements, sometimes collapsed: mines, sand pits, stone, chalk and other mineral quarries. These may have been undisturbed for hundreds or thousands of years. No doubt the peat diggings of east Norfolk were reptile heavens prior to the flooding which created the Norfolk Broads. Old sink holes on limestone, and bomb craters filled with shrubs and grasses, are excellent places for immature reptiles, particularly slow-worms, to feed and grow. Adults may spread away from such places into surrounding grassland or heathland.

Distribution

With an understanding of the preference of reptiles for certain habitats, and armed with what has been documented in historical records, the guessing game as to why reptiles are present or absent in certain areas is slightly easier.

The smooth snake is the rarest British reptile, with the sand lizard close behind and more endangered. Grass snakes are the next species giving cause for concern, followed by adders. The common lizard and slow-worm are the most widespread and abundant. Trying to establish actual numbers of each species is not very easy or meaningful, because population numbers

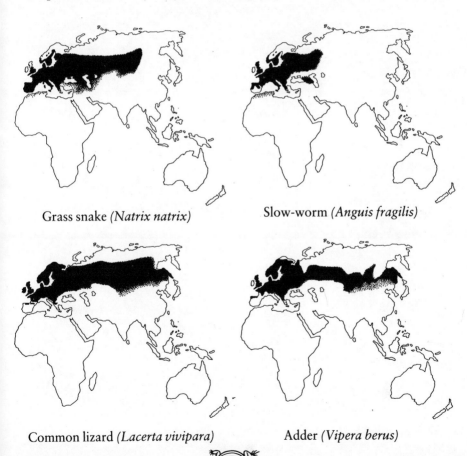

Grass snake *(Natrix natrix)*

Slow-worm *(Anguis fragilis)*

Common lizard *(Lacerta vivipara)*

Adder *(Vipera berus)*

Approximate distribution of reptiles in Britain; the larger areas marked black indicate the localized range of populations, not that they are distributed everywhere within them.

Adder *(Vipera berus)*

Slow-worm *(Anguis fragilis)*

Common lizard *(Lacerta vivipara)*

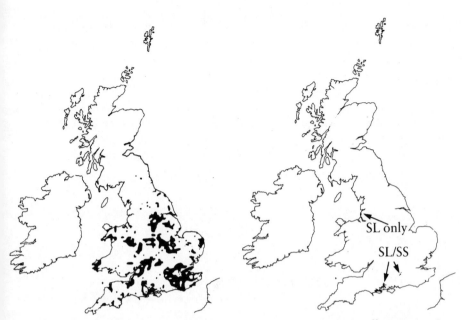

Grass snake *(Natrix natrix)*

Smooth snake *(Coronella austriaca)*
and sand lizard *(Lacerta agilis)*

fluctuate naturally, with peaks and crashes. The most important factor is the number of isolated populations and their rate of loss or increase, rather than the number of individuals within the population at a given site. We are still fairly ignorant about distribution and numbers of reptiles though basic trends have been mapped. The density of reptile sites decreases as you move northwards. The common or viviparous lizard, slow-worm and adder are found on a few of the Hebridean islands off Scotland, but only the common lizard has reached the Isle of Man. The smooth snake is found in one or two outposts beyond the Purbeck hills of Dorset and in adjoining Bagshot woodlands, often on soils next to sandy heaths. Apart from these odd sites, it is confined to the sandy heaths of Dorset, and west Hampshire; a few sites remain on what habitat is left of large exposed beds of sand; on the Bagshot sands to the north and west and Hythe and Lower Greensands to the south of Surrey and eastern Hampshire.

Grass snakes sites are hard to pinpoint, as individuals may range over several miles and in some counties this means that odd snakes may turn up just about anywhere. Records may also be confused by escaped pets. Finding places of key importance for breeding, hibernating or feeding is necessary, and in any local area, a line drawn between these three types of places might crudely pinpoint what could be called a grass snake 'site'. The grass snake is sparsely distributed outside central and south-eastern England; far fewer modern records come from north-west England.

The adder is now very scarce in much of Scotland and central England though little recent survey work has been carried out. It is the most widespread British snake, though populations are fragmented and isolated. Adders are most often recorded from coastal and hilly terrain.

Records show that the sand lizard occurs in the Avon valley where Hampshire joins Dorset, west from there to beyond the Isle of Purbeck,

There are a number of theories as to why snakes are absent from Ireland.

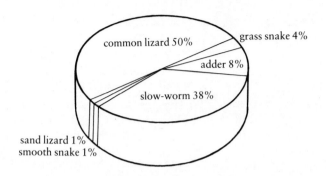

A rough estimate of the relative proportions of the total number of reptile populations remaining in Britain.

and on the heathlands of Surrey and east Hampshire. They are thought to have occurred in the past in some places in the London and Hampshire basins, and southern Berkshire. There are no sites remaining to confirm their past existence in coastal Kent and East Sussex. Colonies on the dune systems north of Liverpool Bay in Merseyside are all that remain from a previous scattering which included colonies along the coastline to the west. Other records are most likely the results of introductions.

The common lizard is the only British reptile to have reached Ireland. Common lizards can be found on islands large and small around the British Isles and are the only reptiles on the Isle of Man. Introductions by humans could in many cases have been the method of colonization, though this may be hard to prove.

Slow-worms are quite widespread, though are found on fewer islands. Records suggest highest numbers in southern England, with a marked decline in records as you move through northern England into Scotland.

Cold blood

Being cold-blooded is one of the aspects of reptile life that adds (unfairly) to their notoriety. It means that the animal must absorb heat from the surrounding environment rather than providing it internally as its main source of energy; behaviour, body shape and coloration must all be geared to this. In sheltered places during sunny weather it is possible for snakes and lizards to heat up quite quickly beyond air temperature.

The raising of body temperature from within by small amounts without an external source of heat in reptiles is only possible with high oxygen consumption and considerable loss of fat reserves and body weight.

The evolution of snakes and lizards — and other animals for that matter — can be compared to the design of cars. Some of the more successful models stay around and maybe change only a little from time to time, while obsolete or less efficient versions may suddenly become unsuitable and quickly disappear. So a snake with a simple but effective design for living may last unchanged for ages, while other types of animal such as warm-blooded mammals may whizz through designs that take the world by storm.

Reptiles today are a reminder of a great 120-million-year long era when reptile life dominated the earth. Towards the end of this period and prior to the much debated dinosaur extinctions, dinosaurs and other orders of reptile-like animals began to decline in numbers. For one reason or another they were unable to survive changes to their environment. It is generally thought that these changes were global rather than local. One theory is that a giant meteor crashed into the earth causing climatic and other changes dinosaurs were unable to survive. Natural selection may simply have favoured new types of animals. Whatever the reason, the result was that these animals of such large sizes were unable to continue to roam the earth.

Fossil records for snakes and lizards are by no means complete. Snakes are thought to have evolved from lizards at about the time of the dinosaur extinctions, and we have evidence of the existence of snakes which resemble modern boas from this period.

The last big reptile show

Many people today may never have seen a British reptile, altough a few can relate stories from their youth in the 1940s and 50s when reptiles were more abundant. Sand lizards, for example, were so common between the 1940s and early 1960s on the Lancashire sand dunes that they were collected in large numbers by visiting schoolchildren and were sold in Liverpool's pet shops.

We have already seen how the reptiles flourished and were then restricted by natural closing up of the tree canopy prior to Neolithic clearance. What has happened in the last few decades to so permanently reduce the abundance of these animals? To start with, the familiar story of human population growth and the demands of cities on our countryside. Building of houses, roads and factories has also taken its toll: fertile land has been reserved for crops, so building has concentrated on heathlands. Scrubby, marginal land has been brought into production, firstly by the war effort, and secondly by the intensification of agriculture encouraged by the Common Agricultural Policy in Europe. The planting of trees such as fast-growing conifers on poorer sandy soils has in many places smothered heathlands with a green shroud, particularly in Dorset. Upland heather moors, with their little pockets of less disturbed heather and bracken are more intensively burnt and grazed, and Scotland now bears the brunt of subsidized tree planting.

In large open areas such as the New Forest, the numbers of visitors, over-grazing and fires create open areas, but also cause disturbance so that few reptiles but the common lizard thrive.

Little pockets of snakes and lizards remain in isolation. In the past, military establishments enclosed considerable tracts of marginal land, yet now they protect these areas from other negative effects, and due to sympathetic management there are important sanctuaries on military land. Extractions of sand and gravel have also taken their toll and continue to do so as a result of planning permissions granted decades ago.

In towns and suburbs, domestic cats kill snakes and lizards, particularly the latter. Small colonies may be hunted-out from isolated banks and churchyards by zealous cats. There can be similar effects from children and adults, though killing and collecting is, we hope, largely a thing of the past. In a recent incident I was called to an uproar in several adjoining suburban gardens. The fear of snakes caused one garden owner to sunbathe in a deckchair wearing a pair of Wellington boots and with a loaded airgun by her side. The previous occupiers had built a low south-facing rubble rockery, covered with a light soil; a superb hibernation and basking area for the four species of commoner reptile.

Dry brittle heather and grass is prone to fire and we have seen dry years where huge fires have cleared large tracts of land. Reptile numbers crash on these sites; either they are burnt in the fire or, afterwards, are easily picked off by predators. Usually a few escape through edge areas to form stock to recolonize in later years, though this is more difficult in small isolated areas. We do not have the large areas of continuous vegetation that buffered the effects of fires. These days fires are often started by careless passers-by, dropping cigarette ends, for example, rather than by lighting strike. The gassing of mammal burrows (see 'Hibernation and emergence') has thoughtlessly damaged and even wiped out reptile populations over the years and should not be overlooked as a major cause of reptile depletion.

In addition to these indirect attacks by humans, direct persecution has been a major influence on population numbers. A few years ago, a televised ramble included the beating to death of an adder with a stick. There are dozens of publicized killings of snakes, which are usually called adders though frequently they are slow-worms or grass snakes, sometimes with the blessing or help of policemen or local politicians who no doubt see their actions as demonstrations of their concern for the public and possibly symbolic purging of evil.

Killing snakes was common in the last century. In the 1860s, for example, at a Scottish loch-side 2,400 adders were reportedly killed on a large estate

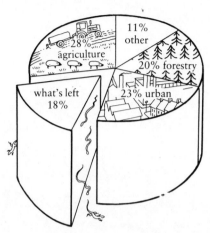

What's left of dry lowland heathland in Britain, after Moore (1962).

over a ten-year period. While populations then could perhaps withstand culls, over the last few decades it has become apparent that smaller colonies of snakes and the snake-like slow-worm have been beaten to extinction. Snake bashing was a traditional Victorian pastime for farm labourers and estate workers. Incidents are getting less common, but sadly this is more because there are fewer snakes rather than because of a change of attitude. However, golf-course managers, gamekeepers, fish-pond owners and others are increasingly aware that snakes should be left alone and not become the target of a killing frenzy. I have only once seen a group of humans killing a snake. The bloodthirsty chase and kill was by what could be best described as a 'pack' of picnickers whose brutality towards a grass snake resembled a primeval ritual.

The British population has recently begun to increase its concern for the problems of our changing environment as can be seen from the 7% of the population who are now subscribers to nature conservation organizations of some kind. The statistics are grim. It is too late to save many of the reptile strongholds in Britain. Almost 80% of dry lowland heathland in Britain, including much of the famous area featured in the novels of Thomas Hardy, have been lost since 1750. In 1811, heathlands covered an almost continuous block on the tertiary sands of Dorset. From 1822—1960 this was reduced from 34,000, to 11,000 hectares, while over a similar period, the Surrey heaths crashed from 50,000 hectares to just 7,500. In Merseyside there has been massive degradation of one stronghold for sand lizards, a place once famed for its beauty and wildlife. Between

Southport and the river Alt, 62% of the large ancient dune system has been built upon or modified between 1801 and 1979. Sand extraction for building, and reduction in rabbit grazing because of myxomatosis, a lowering of the water table and recreational pressures from hundreds of thousands of holiday-makers have taken their toll. Losses of marginal land and meadows have had dramatic effects on the commoner species, too. These may result in smaller populations with local extinction an ever-present threat.

Between 1970 and 1980 there was an alarming reduction of 73% in the number of sand lizard colonies in Dorset from 166 to 44. Partly this must have been due to fires which in 1976 swept through 11% of Dorset's remaining heathland, including 25—30% of areas over 10 years old and leaving only 5% of heaths older than 20 years. From 1965—75 the number of sand lizard colonies near Frensham in Surrey crashed from 56 to just 2. All 22 of the New Forest sand lizard sites are now gone, the result of over-grazing, over-burning, new roads and recreational pressures. Sand lizard numbers are judged in terms of numbers of adults. In 1977, one estimate suggested a national figure of only 7,500 adults: most in Dorset, and 200 in Merseyside, 550 in Surrey, 120 on the Hampshire/Dorset border, and 150 on sites where lizards had been reintroduced (See Translocations). About 85% of the Dorset dry lowland heathlands are currently 'protected' as Sites of Special Scientific Interest and 27% of these are in conservation ownership.

Snake worship

The Christian use of the serpent to represent the devil has been enshrined in an annual ceremony in the little mountain town of Cucullo in Italy. 'The procession of the snakes' takes place on the first Thursday of May each year to commemorate Saint Dominic, a travelling preacher who set out to conquer the Reformist movements in the 13th century. The reformists were disliked for their criticism of religious ritual and their attacks on the clergy as being part of the wealthy ruling classes. The reformists were commonly referred to as snakes and St Dominic is often depicted with a subdued snake.

During the ceremony at Cucullo, a wooden statue of St Dominic is adorned with locally caught climbing snakes (four-lined and Aesculapian) which sit, unable to escape, around the head and shoulders of the life-size statue. This is then held by four bearers and accompanied by church followers and the local community through the town. Saint Dominic is reported to have once been bitten by a snake and not to have suffered any effects. Followers believe that they get protection from the venom of asps (adder-like vipers) which are found in the fields around Cucullo.

Snakes are worshipped in many places outside Europe — though such traditions are breaking down. In the south-west USA American tribes such as Pomo, Yukits and Hopi Indians worship snakes as representatives of their ancestors and may engage in ritual dances with live rattlesnakes. There are also snake-handling sects amongst immigrant Americans. West African snake worship extended to the keeping of large pythons and a prohibition on harming them on pain of death. In south-east Asia, Japan, Nepal, Australia and many other places there are examples of snake temples and snake cults.

Snakes are worshipped as symbols of power and gods; the cobra, for example, is a sacred animal in the Hindu religion. In some cases snakes are phallic symbols and important in human puberty and fertility rituals and events. They may also represent immortality, knowledge and healing as well as more negative images of fear, sin and death. There can be little doubt that snakes have had a powerful significance for human civilization.

Habitat management

Since it is clear that wildlife can no longer rely on slowly adjusting to man's changes of land use, we need to consider special measures to allow species to continue to exist. This is often called habitat management and requires an attitude very different from that of producing as many crops as possible. When we manage for reptiles, we are managing for the whole animal and plant community, in order to sustain more than just a string of fenceless zoos. As well as considering nature reserves, the managing of forestry rides, embankments of motorways and railways and other parts of the wider countryside is going to be vital in a rational strategy to protect British wildlife.

Part of the problem of planning a future for reptiles is that habitat management should be co-ordinated and heathland management can be

Forestry rides can make good reptile habitats as long as they are sufficiently wide to avoid shading by the crop. Extractions should be carried out carefully when the trees are felled to minimize disturbance. The spraying of chemicals and rabbit burrow gassing should also be avoided.

a controversial subject. The mosaic of uneven-aged plants in dry lowland heathland is what reptiles require; this heterogeneous jungle is the result of a cycle of grazing, fire and natural plant death which was the natural course of events over the last two thousand years until recently. These cycles would have been on a massive scale with huge fires, yet rapid recolonization due to the abundance of animals and plants. We are now left with the task of carefully trying to mimic these massive effects on the remaining fragments. One view is to stop all burning, as it is too risky, and to concentrate on very selective turf stripping and mechanical cutting. Another view is to prevent scrub from encroaching, and this may be easiest where the habitat is already of uneven age. On newly burnt areas the efforts to create uneven age artificially should be started as early as possible.

Habitat management requires skilled application. The planning of habitat management, the methods of cutting, felling and removing trees and scrub, the use of selective herbicides and machinery are all forms of what might be best described as an art that requires careful execution. A 'national' policy

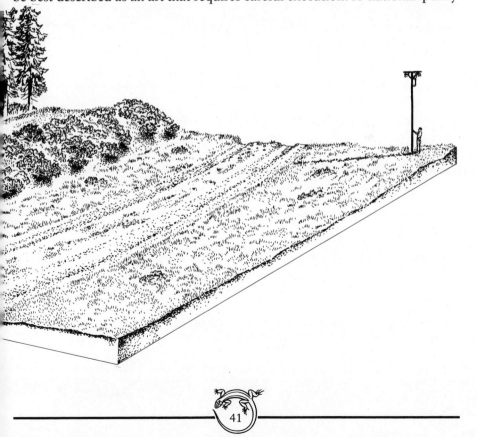

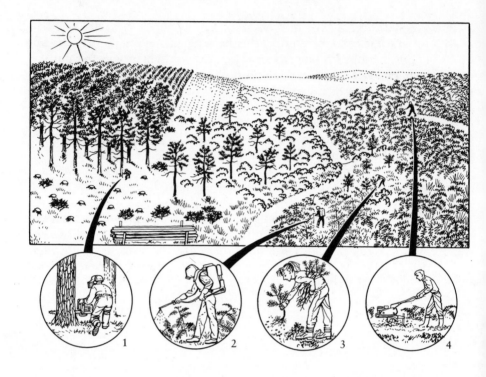

Repairing the heathland landscape: (above) *before and* (opposite) *after.*

1. *Changing forestry practice includes better design of plantations, removal of old, failed crops and zoning of areas big enough to sustain all heathland plants and animals.*

2. *Controlling the spread of bracken with careful use of chemicals. Cutting and spraying methods can help recover ground, particularly those otherwise swamped by the tall, dense bracken monoculture after a fire.*

3. *The spread of seedling pines from plantations can be a recurring problem.*

4. *Creating paths and fire breaks is important on vulnerable, dry heathlands. The risk from uncontrolled fires is greatest during long spells without rain.*

exists for the creating of fire-breaks, for fire control around sites of high reptile density and for the cutting back of gorse from the edges of fire-breaks. Such forward thinking runs ahead of practical implementation which is often sadly lacking. Voluntary groups know what is needed but cannot afford to act, while government spends to reduce the current rate of habitat decline and has little over to keep what is protected worth protecting. On a local basis, the improvement of micro-habitats for reptiles has been relatively successful. The creation of open sand patches for sand lizards, for example, may greatly boost numbers, and clearing south-facing slopes of invading pine has kept larger areas viable for reptile occupation. All is not yet lost.

Lounge lizard

Reptiles bask to gain heat, but there are other important processes beyond just warming up. Vitamin production in skin is one function. There are in addition all the internal demands that other animals may meet by using their internally generated heat. While lizards may rarely be active after dusk, in hot weather the early evening activity of snakes out hunting is more often reported. Each species of reptile has its own preferred temperature: for example, a sand lizard and a common lizard the same size which live in the same habitat, may have different body temperatures. This may partly be due to one species having a larger average adult size. The bigger a lizard is, the smaller its surface area compared to its bulk and the longer it will take to warm up. Its heating system may need to be quicker to get the advantage of smaller lizards. Reptiles are often below ground for more than half of their 'active' season. On some days they may sit at the entrance to a burrow with their heads exposed, but it will not be warm enough for them to emerge.

As well as direct sunshine, air (shade) temperature and ground temperature are important in determining when reptiles may be active. Flattening of the body to increase the surface area exposed to direct sunshine and reduce that exposed to breezes is one technique used by snakes and lizards. This reduces the cooling effects of breezes and is assisted by the spreading and flattening of the rib cage and, in legged lizards, the spreading of feet. Snakes often coil up into a circular or oval shape at low temperatures to reduce the heat loss from what would otherwise be a large surface area. Adders may spread their ribs and flatten themselves to an extent that looks almost impossible.

Snakes and lizards may emerge quite early in the day. Common lizards

Body-flattening in the sun will speed warming up.

are out earliest and at lower temperatures than any other reptiles. They indulge in prolonged late afternoon basking between about 4 and 6 p.m., particularly on rock and log surfaces.

The preferred body temperature in common lizards has been measured at about 30°C. Sand lizards may be out an average of roughly one hour longer than common lizards on sunny afternoons, though common lizards have been out earliest in the morning. Sand lizard daily activity is mostly from 8 a.m. until 7 p.m. Adults emerge earlier and spend more time basking than juveniles, which are more active. Body temperature of active sand lizards may vary from about 12° to 35°C (the average is 25.3°C). One single-season study of a sand lizard colony in Merseyside found them active from 6 a.m. until 10 p.m. Peak activity was recorded around 11 a.m. and 6 p.m.

Adders are rarely out before air temperatures reach 10°C and normally appear at about 13°C. Grass snakes are a little less cold tolerant, not emerging until air temperatures reach 15°C. In very hot weather, however, grass snakes may be seen out early and sit high in hedges to warm up. They may have warmed up sufficiently by 8 a.m. and not be easily seen after this. Smooth snakes may have a body temperature of 26°C by mid-afternoon.

Losing as well as gaining heat may be important and a form of dog-like panting by lizards has been reported by one observer. Snakes and lizards do not have sweat glands in their skin and so cannot cool down in the same way as humans, but their skin may exude oils, and this may have some limited cooling effect. They do however have a capacity to absorb water through the skin.

Aestivation

During the active season, conditions for reptiles can get too hot and dry (yes, even in Britain!). During dry conditions with daytime temperatures consistently above about 21°C in the shade, adders may disappear into the ground, and then, in turn, grass snakes and smooth snakes will find conditions too difficult for them to remain at the surface. As reptiles, particularly lizards, may not get much chance to drink, the risks of dehydration during hot, dry conditions are considerable, and periods of summer dormancy (known as 'aestivation') of many weeks may bring a number of advantages provided they are not so long as to interfere with other life processes.

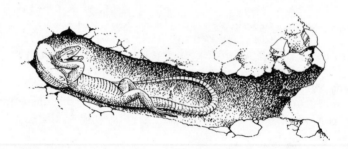

Organization

Lizards and snakes may look very different (though don't forget the slow-worm is a lizard) but in fact there are many similarities due to their common ancestry. The lizard generally has a shorter body, usually with four well developed limbs. Movable eyelids are particular to the lizards, as is a shorter, fatter tongue, an external ear and a fused lower jaw. The slow-worm skeleton has indications (or vestiges) of what back in time would have been used as a pelvic girdle, and the skeleton of legged lizards has many similar features to birds' and mammals'. By weight the lizard has a much higher proportion of scales or body armour than a snake. The large European glass lizard, which is legless and resembles the slow-worm, incredibly has a proportionally greater mass of protective covering than the tank-like tortoises of similar climates.

The skeleton and muscle systems of snakes are especially designed to link bones with the outer skin and scales to assist with movement. Snakes may have over 340 vertebrae with the internal organs enclosed within a large number of ribs; there is no protective sternum at the front. Muscles lie and may stretch alongside several ribs in a chain which creates the regular tube shaped appearance.

The mouths of snakes have a wide gape to swallow prey whole. Both sides of the upper and lower jaw can be moved independently and moved backwards and forwards to increase grip and pressure to force food into the gullet. The jaws may eventually dislocate at the hinge to allow really big meals through — and then go back into position. Large fish of 5 cm (2 inch) diameter are probably the fattest meal eaten by the average British

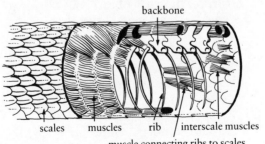

backbone

scales   muscles   rib / interscale muscles

muscle connecting ribs to scales

Scales, muscles and ribs of snakes are arranged to give protection for internal organs and smooth movement along the ground.

grass snake, though the occasional large individual might cram down even bulkier meals.

The snake gullet is very long, up to one third of the total length of the body. It leads into an elongated stomach, which, like the gullet, has a remarkable capacity to stretch when food items are engulfed. The reason for this is that food is eaten whole. The lizard stomach can also swell to take advantage of large quantities of seasonally abundant food. There is a large liver, a gall bladder and pancreas. The digestive system is designed for maximum water retention with excretion of substances like uric acid and urates which resemble bird droppings. These leave the body with undigested bones and other matter through a single vent or cloaca, which also holds the reproductive appendages.

The organs of snakes are long, thin, and sited one in front of the other to fit within the constraints of the body cavity, and often one of a pair is small and almost redundant, for example the left lung. The snake heart has three chambers compared to the mammalian four. In this cruder design a single outgoing chamber or ventricle mixes freshly oxygenated blood from the lungs with that which has passed through the body.

Snakes and lizards are unusual in the reptile world because they have teeth which are fused with the jaw bone rather than being in sockets. Both have nostrils which are positioned at the front of the head and inhale air for breathing and smell. In snakes, the tongue is divided, long and fine pointed. Lizard tongues are notched and blunter. They retract into a fleshy sheath which protects their sensitivity. The reptilian tongue carries particles from the atmosphere onto two ducts on the top of the palate known as Jacobson's Organ. This arrangement of tongue and organ enhances their ability to detect small amounts of scents for sexual recognition, feeding and general inspection of their surroundings.

Snakes have no eardrums or external ears, but the inner ear is connected to the bones of the lower jaw, and is highly sensitive to fine vibration. Sand lizards and common lizards (but not slow-worms) have a dark oval plate on the side of the head and neck called a tympanum. Like an ear, this gathers and amplifies sound and is thought to make for quite acute hearing at short distances and may be important when lizards hunt.

The lizard eye is quite similar to that of mammals except that it has a simplified method of changing the shape of the lens. A ring of bony eye plates around the eye withstand the build-up of pressure to make this possible. Snakes have a strong protective covering to their eyes, much like a large contact lens, which protects them, as does an eyelid. This is called a 'brille' and is renewed when snakes slough. The vision of the British reptiles is relatively limited, more sensitive to movement than anything else and most useful at short distances. Sand lizards have partial colour vision and can differentiate at least eight colours. They are especially sensitive to yellow and green which are the dominant male colours during the breeding season. Reptiles cannot close their eyes, but can rest in a form of sleep when both in the open and under shelter.

During hibernation and aestivation, the reptile body may reduce its heart rate and metabolism for considerable periods. When in the open, the state of readiness to respond to movement, vibration or scent is much greater than when underground. Within a fraction of a second a reptile, which during weeks of sunny weather has basked undisturbed in a favoured spot, may disappear into its surrounds like a sprinter off the blocks.

The limbs of the lizard are jointed and have five fingers and five toes which are hinged in two places and end with a tiny claw. On close inspection they resemble the unwebbed feet of birds, and the back toes can be very fine and flexible. Fingers and toes are sometimes lost during fighting, and in winter from frostbite or fungal attack, though often with no noticeable loss in agility. Some researchers have even clipped the shorter toes off to identify individuals during population studies.

Moving

Snakes move using several different techniques, depending on the species and the ground through which they are moving. Most snakes are good swimmers and climbers and co-ordinate their powerful muscles as a substitute for the absence of legs. Snake muscles run along the body, between ribs, between ribs and scales and between scales.

In most situations, pressure from the underside of the snake is exerted against the ground at a slight angle to the direction in which the snake wishes to go.

This produces momentum and sideways grip for the body which develops the typical serpentine undulating shape. When a snake comes into contact with an object — perhaps a stone or plant stem — this is then used to brace and push itself forward, rippling the muscles against it in a smooth action which often looks completely effortless. For small movements, the snake may stretch out and then pull itself forwards; much in the way a caterpillar moves along a branch, though not to the extent of looping of the body. British snakes can move quite quickly over short distances. One of the fastest snakes, the venomous black mamba, moves extremely fast over short distances, so fast in fact that one circling and investigating my presence while I was walking through a Kenyan forest a few years ago resembled a grey blur, and was gone in a split second.

Legged lizards are able to clamber often using similar methods to fingered and toed mammals. Their legs are jointed and quite adaptable. This allows them to clamber in tangled vegetation to their best advantage and helps them get into good positions for basking, as well as for hunting invertebrates that live higher up. Slow-worms, lacking limbs, have the same problem as snakes but not their dexterity above ground. Though they move in similar fashion, and can move very fast when trying to escape, they are quickly exhausted. This is one reason why they are found hidden for much of the time; they specialize in efficient burrow-making with the use of the powerful head and neck which is pushed forward under great pressure.

'Upon thy belly shalt thou go'

The distribution or range of a population depends on the position of suitable places for hibernation, feeding, breeding, basking and refuge. The relative position of these areas will greatly influence the number of times reptiles come into contact with each other and the intensity of competition. Sand lizards, for example, may be scattered according to variations in small hills and slopes (topography), but the need to have bare sand for egg laying may preclude anything but a few transient individuals in many areas. The home range (the area that an animal uses during its life) of sand lizards has been calculated at a little more than the size of a tennis court. However nine sand lizards of both sexes have been found together in a night refuge, suggesting that they may live close together and have overlapping living areas.

The upper limits of a reptile's home range varies with each reptile. Grass snakes may regularly move five hundred yards and in some cases over a mile in order to feed, breed and hide away. When females need to find a breeding site they may have to travel this far. The average smooth snake movements are thought to be in the region of around 70-80 metres (76-87 yards) with a maximum of about 500 metres (550 yards). They may have a home range of up to three hectares.

Sand lizards and common lizards will stake out territories (small areas within a home range which to some degree are defended) around their burrows, but not slow-worms. Strong aggressive males will keep the good refuges and establish food-finding routes which they patrol and may defend. Later in the year forays up to 36 metres (40 yards) may be made into surrounding habitat. In spring lizards spend more time basking. Emaciated, dead, immature sand lizards have been found at the edge of suitable habitats and exclusion by bullying male sand lizards has been suggested as the cause of this mortality. Females are sometimes allowed to follow the same feeding or patrol routes of dominant males.

The number or density of animals in an area is one way of describing populations. At one thriving colony, the density of grass snakes was found to be around three adults per hectare. Sand lizard colonies are often judged by the numbers found in an area of 100 square metres, about half a tennis court. Ten lizards in this area represents a flourishing colony, with 43 the record. Outside Britain it may exceed 60 individuals in such an area. Smooth snake populations have been measured as varying from about 1 or 2 per hectare to as many as 11-17.

Despite their territoriality, lizards from a single population may cluster together in order to share the best position for basking, though little is known about when, how and why lizards might leave an established territory. In some cases young sand lizards must search for new places away from a dense colony. Even the burrow of a leaf-cutting bee has once been reported as being used as a temporary refuge by a sand lizard.

One study of common lizards suggested that a third of all young perish after their first winter, and that less than half the remainder live to the next winter. By the end of their second winter numbers would be down to a third, when the bigger males will be mature for the first time. So from 100 hatchings, 15 young females survive to face at least a further full season and winter before breeding for the first time in their fourth year. Another study has suggested that 90% of hatchling common lizards die in their first twelve months of life, but that once they have reached this point the remainder will reach an average age of 4 to 5 years. Sand lizard survivorship may be even lower than this with one estimate of 3-4 years as an average life expectancy, with 8-10 years the maximum age of a lucky individual. A detailed study of adders in Dorset suggested an overall toll of 24% of the adder population each year, the main causes being humans and buzzards. Mortality will vary according to predation, competition, disease and factors resulting from topography and other physical constraints of a habitat.

Hibernation and emergence

Reptile 'hibernation' is a state of torpor and inactivity into which snakes and lizards go in winter as a method of solving two problems. Firstly, sunlight hours diminish as the sun moves lower across the horizon, and daytime temperatures drop to below those where activity is easy or possible. Secondly, their prey — small mammals, other reptiles, amphibians and fish — may enter some sort of winter dormancy or reduced activity. Invertebrates are scarce and so food is not easily available. Reptiles must gradually store fat over the active season, in order to have the energy which will be required to produce young. Fat is stored in special places within the body, technically called 'fat bodies' and in other parts of the body such as the tail. Energy is required for courtship and mating during the spring, so sitting tight and shutting down to a low metabolic rate for winter is just about the only option available. In Britain snakes do not always breed every year; some may go two seasons without breeding. The same species may be far more fecund in warmer parts of Europe where the climate is not so limiting. Our north-westerly latitude is on the edge of a combination of climatic factors that limits reptile distribution. The grass snake, for example, does not occur in numbers farther north than northern England despite the availability of what might otherwise seem suitable habitats.

From August, but depending on each species and variable weather patterns, reptiles of different size, sex and age start to make their way below what will become the frost line according to their individual needs. Temperatures below ground vary. During a surface freeze, at a depth of 25cm (10 inches) the temperature is usually about 2°C. At half a metre (1 foot 8 inches) this has risen to 4.5° C. Reptiles may find their way to depths of 2 metres (6 feet 7 inches), often using holes made by tree, gorse and heather roots, and probably deeper when sharing mammal burrows. Female grass snakes are reported to enter hibernation earlier on average than males, starting from late September. By the end of October most are resting in a torpid state.

The dens in which they hibernate may be used as resting places before winter; some sorties are made from hibernating dens before and after the main period of hibernation when reptiles are not fully torpid. During these in-between periods before and after full hibernation, underground battles

Snakes and lizards may emerge during hot, sunny spells in mid-winter.

must be fought for food with both the prey itself and perhaps other occupants, for space to rest safely. In some instances predator and prey must overwinter together.

In a long, mild autumn, reptiles may still be active in November or even December, but there is almost always a four- to six-month period when most individuals are underground. During hot, sunny winter days in sheltered spots reptiles— particularly adders and common lizards — may emerge and bask, often to no ill effect. At other times they may risk being caught out and killed by a snap frost. In a descriptive account of lizards emerging in early spring in his *Lives of British Lizards* Colin Simms observes the disadvantages of being a British lizard: 'part of the trunk, or the hind limbs are sometimes "frozen" and dragged about grotesquely until the lizard has had the opportunity to bask enough to thaw them out. This is particularly noticeable during periods when there are ground frosts.' While the lizards could not have been literally frozen, the condition must be the result of temperatures close to freezing.

Reptiles may overwinter individually or in groups in a place often referred to as a hibernaculum. The groups can be very large: eight hundred adders are reported to have been found hibernating together at one site in Finland. And in this country about sixty smooth snakes have been found together at the site of some old Nissen huts. Lizards and snakes often choose human constructions such as the foundations of old buildings, old railway sleepers, piles of straw and manure, rock piles, banks and hedgerows as hibernation sites. They will also use excavations made by rabbits, foxes and rodents. Old tree stumps may also offer shelter from frost below the surface. Hibernacula are often in high, dry, south-facing places sheltered from north or easterly winds, and away from spots prone to flooding or high humidity. Reptiles are often reported in the media when they congregate in large numbers. One old newspaper cutting tells of a farmer digging out a 'ball' of about twenty slow-worms in a hedge bank rabbit hole. Winter mortality takes a toll on populations. Monitoring of an adder colony suggested that 15% of adult and 30-40% of juveniles may die in hibernation. Similar mortality has been reported in juvenile common lizards and sand lizards. Predation, disease, suffocation, freezing, starvation and 'old age' all may account for deaths. Upon emergence, there may be prolonged basking or lying-out period, which varies amongst individuals; in grass snakes this may last until May. Groups of adders may be seen basking together. Both snakes and lizards may climb low shrubs to a height of up to 4 feet in order to find advantageous basking places.

Snakes and lizards tend to start moving above ground in mid to late March and April in response to increasing day length and higher temperatures; perhaps some form of internal clock also tells them when to emerge. Adult males need to bask in order to mature their sperm, so they usually emerge first. While females' emergence overlaps they are generally later out by a few days. Adult reptiles are often out earlier than juveniles. In Britain, dates of emergence will vary considerably from the warmest parts of south-west England to later emergence in the cooler northern parts and in the same general area topography will create naturally cooler areas. In southern England common lizards and slow-worms usually emerge in mid-March, and sand lizards usually in late March or early April. This is a good time to see snakes and lizards; they can be sluggish.

Communal overwintering of slow-worms.

Snake charming?

The reptile breeding season typically lasts for six weeks from a date when daytime temperatures reach 13-15°C. On emergence the sexes are not immediately attracted to each other, but the behaviour of breeding adults will quite suddenly change to concentrate upon courtship and mating. In some circumstances male adders out first from hibernation may find and mate with females close to their dens as they emerge. The 'dance of the adders' is a form of male rivalry which you will be lucky to see in the wild. The adult males chase around together, then stop with their heads and front third or more of their bodies raised. They sway and push at each other until one is too exhausted to continue and retreats.

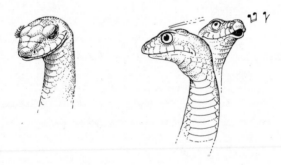

Snakes

Early in the spring male snakes will contest with each other to some degree; adders joust and posture, smooth snakes tussle and male grass snakes will occasionally pose and hiss at each other. Grass snakes and adders may move distances of over a mile to search out females, and couples of all species may bask together as pairs for several days prior to mating. Male reptiles seem to attempt to judge physical receptiveness of females by flicking their tongues over the female's body to assess the body scent. In the adder this may be accompanied by lashing of his tail. Pheromones, or scent from skin and anal glands, play an important role in identification during courtship. Female snakes may announce their presence by brushing against vegetation or by sitting with their vents partially open. The anal glands in adult grass snakes are about two centimetres long. Body oils may play an important role in the final subtleties of mating; as females reach an 'on-heat' state of high fertility males sniff and 'lick' females with their tongues.

Male snakes may rub their chins along the back of females before their

Male adders 'dancing' in spring-time rivalry.

lower halves entwine. Male and female snakes may race together, the female as if trying to escape. When the female tires and stops, the male uses his lower jaw to tap the female. He grips her tail tightly with his tail and mating begins. Snakes and lizards have two penises (called hemipenes) with quite complicated shapes. The simplest is that of the grass snake, while adders are each double tipped and fluted. They are turned inside out on erection and withdrawal, and consist of tubes of erectile tissue turned inside out by the action of muscles and blood. Spines, which may be soft or quite hard according to each species, assist with grip. In most years adders mate in April or May. While autumn matings have been observed in snakes, their success in producing progeny is not clear. It has even been suggested that snakes may in some circumstances mate in their hibernation quarters, but this must be rare. Female snakes may sometimes not respond to courtship, perhaps in years when they are resting and not breeding. Courtship may be quickest in young individuals, becoming more elaborate with age. The pattern of mating is similar in all three species of snake, with the male giving convulsive jerks of his body and persistently tapping his head against the female's body. Grass snakes mate as early as late March but probably mainly during April. Male and female snakes may have several partners, and males may return to a female after she has been mated by others. Smooth snakes mate between March and May, and mating may last for up to fifteen hours.

*A male adder may spend some time 'tasting' the scent of the female
with his tongue prior to mating.*

Male grass snakes may store sperm over winter and thus be able to mate immediately upon emergence. Male grass snakes (and adders) reaching 30cm body length are usually sexually mature. After mating, testis size temporarily increases over the summer in preparation for the following spring. Female grass snakes may start breeding for the first time at about 60cm (24 inches) total body length, but a proportion of individuals in the 60-90cm (24 to 35 inch) band have been found never to have bred. Individuals over 70cm (28 inches) have almost always bred at least once.

Smooth snakes may be noticeably pregnant towards the last days of May, though for late individuals, mating may also occur in that month. Female smooth snakes can be sexually mature at a total body length of 45cm (18 inches).

In Britain, and other cooler parts of northern Europe, snakes do not always breed every year. Female adders breed on average every other year once they have attained a size in excess of 42cm (16 inches). Female smooth snakes may breed in successive years but sometimes only every two or three years. It would seem that grass snakes are the only ones to breed regularly every year, though variation in places with different amounts of food and basking opportunity may cause local effects.

There is a lot more to be learnt about the breeding behaviour of snakes in Britain. It is rarely observed and detailed long-term studies of wild populations would be needed to see how snakes meet, select their mates and breed.

Lizards

Sand lizard males can become very territorial and aggressive to other males. Defence of a territory involves displaying and, on the rare occasion when fighting occurs, it can be fierce and involve bloodshed and wounding. Males may become bright green prior to mating. During more normal confrontations, male sand lizards will stand off, perhaps just a few inches away from each other. By inflating their lungs, they can puff out their necks and upper bodies, and the two lizards display at each other. This may be accompanied by hissing and then butting lunges at the head and shoulder. Exaggerated posturing, with arched backs, bodies raised high on all fours and twitching tails may also be observed. During confrontations the lizards' mouths may be held open and they may bite and seize one another and roll until one submits. Fingers and toes may be broken or lost during such skirmishes. Fighting is not so aggressive between common lizards. They contest and mate in a similar manner to sand lizards but there seems to be less social interaction and territories are less well defined. There is little or no total exclusion of other lizards from an area (territorial bullying), which in sand lizards may involve persistent rejection of an individual. Once a male sand lizard has paired with a female he will bask together with her. Both sexes of sand lizard are promiscuous and mating occurs from April to June, mostly in May.

Sand lizards often copulate after bouts of tail chasing, when the male, checking the scent of the female with flicking tongue, eventually bites and holds onto her flank. Mating scars on the neck and flanks of females may last for months afterwards. The male's grip is moved steadily up towards the female's head and the body bends in a semi-circle to assist with the

Sand lizards mating.

insertion of one of two penises (called hemipenes) according to which side the male is holding on. Mating may last for up to three hours. The male testis are positioned at the base of the tail and cause a noticeable thickening at that point. Common lizards mate in April and early May. The process is similar to that of sand lizards, but mating occurs more sporadically for 5-35 minutes or so. The first females become visibly pregnant in mid-May by which time males are feeding to make up for weight lost due to their long fast during hibernation and courtship and mating. Females take dew and other liquid but do not feed, instead putting last autumn's fat reserves to work.

Slow-worm mating occurs in April, May or June. Contests and rivalry are seldom recorded from the wild, but have been observed in captive animals. Slow-worms couple and mate for many hours, the female's head and neck held in the male's jaws, which sometimes leaves a scar. Despite their serpentine body shape, in lizard fashion the male's body is held in a semi-circle. Lizards are thought to breed every season, though no doubt resting seasons may occur in some circumstances. On very rare occasions two clutches of young in one year may be possible, though in Britain multiple clutching (seen on the Continent) is thought to occur only in captivity.

Egg race

Common lizards are the only British reptiles that are live bearing, or 'viviparous'. Young develop within the body until birth, when they are fully formed, and at birth may together weigh almost half the mother's weight. Pregnancy may last for about twelve weeks.

'Oviparity', or egg laying, is the reproductive method used by sand lizards and grass snakes. The developing embryos are surrounded by an eggshell and then deposited in as secure a place as possible to continue their development prior to hatching. The third category, used by slow-worms, smooth snakes and adders is that of 'ovo-viviparity'. This is the retention of independently developing embryos within the body prior to birth. A thin, opaque or clear membrane called a 'pellicle' is formed around each embryo which then ruptures on birth or soon afterwards. This has the disadvantage of viviparity for the adult females in that they become large and weighed down by young some weeks before birth. It has the advantage that reptiles can breed under conditions which do not favour egg laying, assisting life in cooler northerly latitudes or at higher altitudes on mountains. This for example allows adders to exist within the Arctic circle, though the shortness of the summer means that a two-year gestation period is required. Retention of developing young through winter may also occur in northern England and Scotland.

Sperm storage is the retention of sperm in the reproductive systems of both male and female snakes and lizards for longer periods than usual. This allows fertilization outside normal mating periods and is something that has implications for the study of mate selection and sperm competition. For grass snakes and sand lizards, finding a suitable place to lay your eggs is important and they spend considerable effort and energy doing so. Sand lizards dig test burrows; on average about three are rejected — sometimes as many as eight times—before a suitable one is used for laying. Sand lizard females may occasionally lay together in a particularly suitable burrow. What the lizards are looking for is a suitable soil under the surface: open, disturbed sandy areas are good especially those unshaded and free from plant roots which may cause damage to eggs. Sand lizards generally lay eggs on slopes, or level ground at the base of a slope. They use their heads to dig, with eyes closed, and, bracing on their hind feet and tail, use their forearms to sweep and flick sand backwards to create a hole. The sides of the excavation are pressed firm with the body and the limbs are also

Female sand lizards may dig several test burrows to determine the most suitable place for laying her eggs.

used to pack out and enlarge the inside of the tunnel. After about 15cm (6 inches), they will form a bed to one side of the tunnel. Eggs are laid by the females in this part of the tunnel which is then back-filled with sand to protect and hide the nest. Eggs are usually laid towards the end of June and the first weeks of July. Weather conditions will influence egg laying, and cloudy, wet weather may not favour egg development, particularly in July and August when it may considerably reduce that year's recruitment.

Sand lizard eggs vary in colour from a pearl pink to creamy white or pale grey. When first laid they are about 10-12mm in length, some are 'egg' shaped while others are long and thin, others almost round. These increase by about 5mm in length during incubation, as they absorb moisture and stretch to accommodate the growing embryo. In Britain sand lizards do not have the climatic luxury of their southern neighbours where eggs may be deposited in a wider range of materials; here they must be very choosy. In England the average depth at which sand lizard clutches are found is 7.2cm (3 inches). The best (optimum), temperature would seem to be close to 32°C though this is seldom achieved in the wild in Britain. From six to twelve weeks will usually be required for sand lizard egg incubation in the wild, with hatchlings emerging through the sand in August and September. In egg-laying reptiles whole clutches tend to fail rather than odd ones. Grass snake studies suggest that every degree increase in temperature takes one day off the incubation time. The average incubation time is ten weeks. A clutch laid late in July or August may have little chance of hatching at less than 20°C and in some years recruitment must be quite low with eggs not developing before winter and never hatching.

Grass snakes will lay eggs in a variety of places where warm, humid conditions prevail. Rotting vegetation that naturally accumulates on river banks and piles of farmyard refuse have probably served as important nesting habitats for many centuries. The straw and dung piles of farms and stables and grass compost heaps around sports grounds and parks were often reported as places where grass snakes were abundant during Victorian times. The foundations and wall of buildings are also used; in one place forty batches of eggs were reported in a single crevice. Sawdust heaps, usually created by rural saw-mills, were important places until demand for sawdust increased and undisturbed stacks became rare. Disused mammal burrows are other places where grass snakes will lay eggs. In the process of egg laying, female grass snakes push with the body to make a small cavity. In this cavity the eggs are laid at intervals of four or five minutes. The entire process may take about two hours. A mucus cements the eggs together in a tight bundle. Each egg measures about 24mm (1 inch) by 15mm (0.6 inch), is white, with a thin leathery texture. In 1985 the Fauna and Flora Preservation Society carried out a grass snake survey which investigated the types of artificial egg-laying materials used by grass snakes. The results showed that garden compost heaps, particularly those with high grass content, are the most frequently discovered sites, though more natural places such as under rotting logs were also used. Grass snake eggs have been reported found in pads of moss, collapsed dead bracken, amongst tree roots and in loose soil. Any source of artificial heat seems to be preferred and sewage farms and rubbish tips are also places to which grass snakes may be attracted, particularly as their agricultural refuges diminish. Choice of egg-laying site is important, as eggs may be quickly killed by cold weather; places like

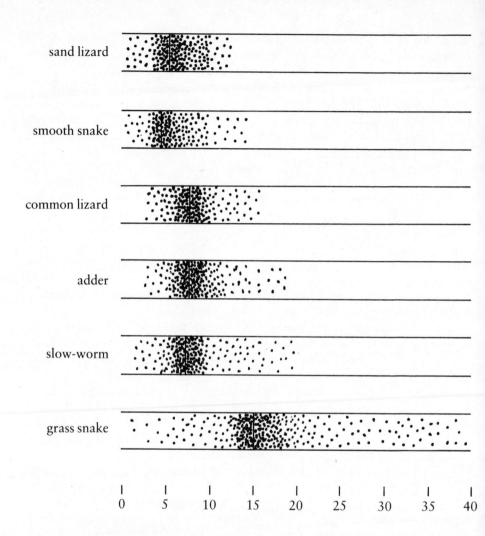

The clutch sizes of British reptiles, showing approximate range of eggs laid or young born, and the number in a 'typical' clutch.

piles of rotting sawdust may be as warm as 28° — 40°C. Grass snakes lay eggs in isolated batches or in communal nests. A report from Russia tells of 1,200 eggs being found under a discarded door, and the record seems to be a count of over 6,000 eggs in one place. The numbers of eggs a female lays is determined by her size — quite literally, how many her body can hold. Very large, old females can manage 40 eggs and there are records from an individual found elsewhere in the grass snake's range of an amazing 73 eggs.

The date on which grass snakes' eggs are laid is determined by the date of fertilization, the delay being about ten weeks. The last batches are laid in mid-October,though hatching beyond mid-November must be very rare.

Grass snake just prior to egg-laying.

Young ones

Hatching of young grass snakes and sand lizards occurs when the fully developed embryo uses an egg tooth at the front of the mouth to break through the thin but tough outer eggshell. Sitting still in the ruptured egg sometimes for over a day, the egg sac begins to be finally absorbed and then detaches, either from the inside of the egg or at the join with the body; usually the egg sac trails from the belly. This soon shrivels and the umbilical scar remains visible for only a short while. Reptiles quickly learn to move. The size of the offspring is not always proportional to the size of its egg. Often eggs will hatch within a few hours of each other. Grass snake young may disperse rapidly from communal egg-laying sites and give rise to stories of plagues of snakes. Sand lizards also disperse quickly and are often hard to find the following spring though this could partly be due to predation and lack of survival through the first winter; they are only about ½ gm in weight and up to 6 cm (2½ inches) long at birth.

Adders, smooth snakes and slow-worms are ovo-viviparous and usually give birth quite late in the year. Smooth snakes are born in late August or early September after a twelve-week gestation period. Following cooler summers, birth may be delayed until October or even November. The mother gives birth to thin, enclosing sacs called pellicles; it may then take up to five hours for the young to release themselves from these. The head and limbs are used to test the pellicle for weak spots.

Common lizards are the only British reptiles that are live bearing or 'viviparous'. Young develop within the body until birth, when they are fully formed, and at birth may together weigh almost half the mother's weight. Pregnancy may last for about twelve weeks.

Common lizards are born over a few hours and sometimes scattered by the female some distance apart. The young are soon strong and active. They are usually born in late June and July but also through until early September, while July and August are the most frequently reported months in northern England. In less favourable conditions common lizards sometimes give birth to slightly incomplete embryos in thin shells which are apparently tough and quite like that of a sand lizard. These measure about 11 mm by 8 or 9 mm. This has been reported at high altitudes (2,700 metres above sea level) in the Haute Pyrenees and Massif Central.

Slow-worms are born from July to October, usually in late August or early September in southern Britain, and August and September in northern

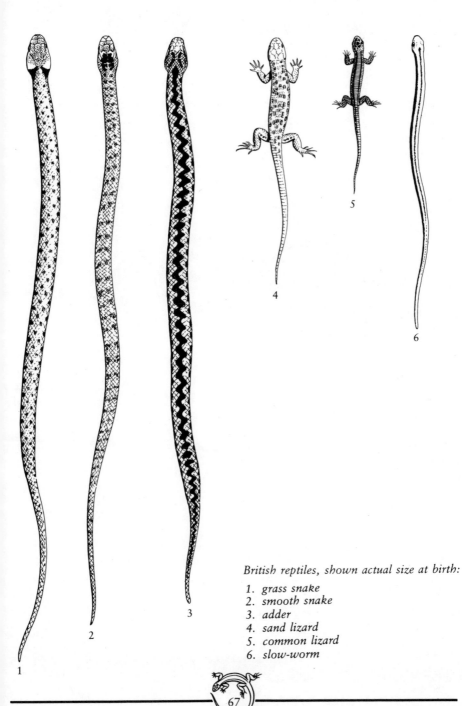

British reptiles, shown actual size at birth:

1. grass snake
2. smooth snake
3. adder
4. sand lizard
5. common lizard
6. slow-worm

Britain. Slow-worms usually have at least a twelve-month pregnancy, sometimes longer, releasing themselves from the pellicle at birth with the help of an egg tooth.

Once they are born, reptiles have little time to explore and feed before it is time to hibernate. In some cases this can be as little as a few weeks or even a few days before the first risks of October frosts. The success of young in the period before hibernation may be important in survival the next year. The common lizard has the smallest hatchlings, but these are born earlier than sand lizards, so have more time to feed prior to winter. Sand lizards measure about 75 mm (3 inches) and weigh 3 gm after their first winter.

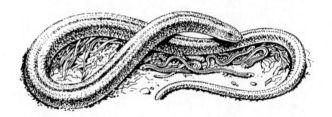

Slow-worm giving birth.

Growth and development

It is worth considering the terminology describing how old an animal is when it matures. An animal is one year old when it reaches January, so an animal in its second calendar year may be less than twelve months old. Male smooth snakes, for example, may mature for the first time in their fourth year or fourth calendar year when about three years old (from birth). Male slow-worms may first mature at a length of about 25 cm (10 inches) in their third or fourth year while females mature and breed for the first time when four or five years old. Terminology can be confusing! In both sand lizards and common lizards, sexual maturity is reached in males usually when two years old and females when they are three years old. Therefore males can breed in the second spring after their birth, females the third. This is the earliest date however, and some may not breed for several years.

Measuring growth in reptiles can be tricky, because it is not easy to recapture the same individuals after periods in large numbers. Snakes may grow at different rates, and the tail may grow at a different rate to that of the body. Rate of growth probably depends on a number of factors, for example how good the weather is during the first year of growth, and

The life cycles of reptiles in the British Isles (after M. Smith, *British Amphibians and Reptiles*, 1951)

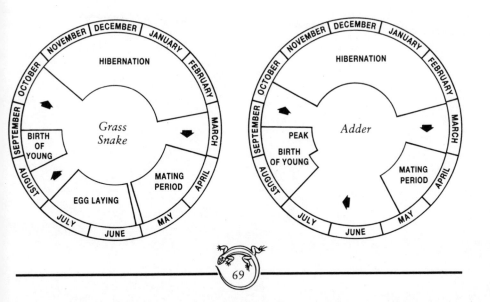

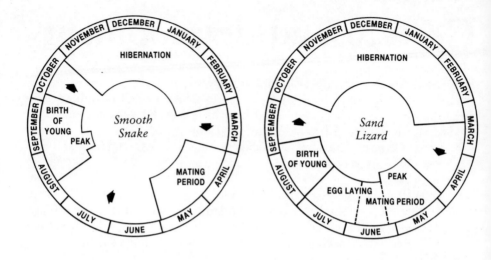

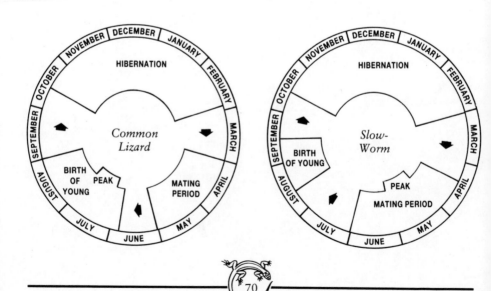

the availability of food. In any one year growth may be repressed, particularly in females, by reproductive activity, which uses up reserves that would other wise be put into growth.

Grass snakes have been measured growing in length by between 20 and 80 mm (¾ - 3 inches) per year. Adders are thought to grow most rapidly in the year following their second hibernation; growth slows considerably after their fourth hibernation. Females of both snakes and lizards mature later than males.

Slough, slough, quick, quick, slough

House dust is partly composed of human skin, which continually falls away from our bodies in tiny flakes, so that we are unaware that it's happening. In reptiles, however, the process of skin shedding occurs all at once, when the entire skin is lost whole or in several pieces. You might be forgiven for thinking that this is a process brought on by sunburn caused by long periods of sunbathing without a sunscreen! In fact the process allows for growth in the outer scales which allows them to catch up with internal growth. It also disposes of dirt, parasites and other unwanted materials on the reptile's skin, and gives the reptile a brighter, new appearance. Sloughs, pronounced 'sluffs', are largely colourless, opaque and cellophane-like, and made mostly of keratin (the hard component of hair and fingernails).

Sloughs are often found in the wild by reptile watchers and are an indication of reptiles in an area. Slow-worm sloughs have uniform small scales and are usually found only in small circular fragments. Legged lizard slough fragments are usually a strip from the head and upper body on which a very faint impression of the body pattern is discernible. If you are lucky enough to find a head slough, look for the imprint of three small scales in a triangular arrangement behind each nostril which will indicate that it belonged to a sand lizard. Three scales in a row would indicate a common lizard. The double-check is that the fifth chin scale should be half the size of the fourth; the common lizard's should be of similar size. Snake sloughs show the single ventral or belly scales, while lizards have rows of ventrals. Adder sloughs reveal the characteristic zig-zag pattern when held to the light and the many small scales on the head and body are also indicative. The body scales of adders and grass snakes are keeled — there is a ridge running along the length of each scale. The imprint of smooth snake scales

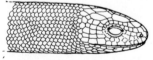 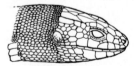 

Outline of lizard head sloughs: (left) *slow-worm* (middle) *sand lizard and* (right) *common lizard*

shows them to be unkeeled. Behind the eye is the image of only two postocular scales (see illustration) is present. Grass snake sloughs have keeled scales, and three postoculars behind the eye.

Reptiles slough one or more times a year depending on their species and age. One of the signs that sloughing is beginning is that the body colour becomes dull. The body and eyes of snakes look cloudy when the old skin is freed from the new by a separating fluid before the slough. Moist conditions are favourable for the old skin to break around the head when moved against objects that give resistance. It is then slowly rubbed and rolled like a stocking inside out down the body. Lizard sloughs break in several pieces because of their arms and legs.

Males generally slough twice each year, and most individuals seem to do it in May and August. Females seem to slough less frequently in the wild but there is little information on this. In gravid females sloughing is

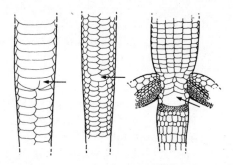

Scale arrangements on the underside of the lower abdomen and upper tail of (left) a snake, (middle) a slow-worm and (right) a legged lizard. The arrows indicate the scale covering the opening of the vent. In snakes this may be a single or double (divided) scale as shown here.

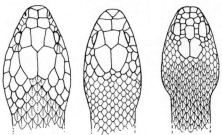

Outline of snake head scales on sloughs: (left) grass snake (middle) smooth snake and (right) adder

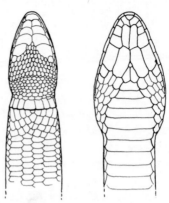

Underside of sloughed reptile skins: (left) *legged lizard* (right) *snake.*

usually just before egg laying at the end of June. Common lizards go in for sloughing in a big way, getting rid of an average of four skins a year. Youngsters, who are growing fast, may do so as many as six times.

In fact when very young snakes and lizards shed their skins often because they grow so fast in the early stages. I have known juvenile smooth snakes slough just a few days after birth and once again after just a further week or so. Slow-worms may slough within four days of hatching, and common lizards and sand lizards may slough two or three times before their first hibernation. More frequently sloughing is observed in warmer countries where growth may be faster. Smooth snakes can be seen in their pre-slough condition between the first week of May and the first week of September. The sloughing process usually takes about 11 to 15 days but one sloughing has been recorded as dragging on for 44. One female smooth snake was recorded sloughing at least twice in one year. Sand lizards are thought to slough about every four to six weeks, and in total up to six or seven times each year. One study suggests that adders slough on average twice per year, the first slough most often in April, the last some time in August. Snakes and lizards may regularly shed the skin from the surface of their tongues, though this is a fine sheet of cells rather than the crisp body slough.

Long life

The maximum age, or longevity, of reptiles often fascinates people, although wild animals are almost always killed by predators before turning up their toes (or tails) naturally. In the wild, smooth snakes have been recorded aged 18 or 19 years, while captive slow-worms seem to get the record at 33—35 years in captivity. However 54 years has been claimed for a European slow-worm. Adders clock in at 15—25 years, grass snakes at 20 years (in captivity), and while sand lizards average only about 5 years in the wild, captives have exceeded the age of 12. The point is that reptiles have the capacity to live much longer than most birds and mammals of similar weight, and this may be important in their ability to hang on and colonize or recolonize after fires or changes in vegetation. The age of a population of reptiles is therefore well worth taking into account when trying to conserve them. Reptiles may be around for some years or even decades after changes to habitats but they may not be reproducing, and declines of numbers in an area may be slow and gradual over twenty or thirty years.

Prey

Grass snakes feed on all amphibians: common toads, natterjack toads, frogs, great crested newts, smooth newts and palmate newts. Amphibian tadpoles and hatchlings are a favourite food. They also feed on fish from streams and ponds — roach, minnows and sticklebacks — and may inspect your garden pond for delicacies of imported origin, such as goldfish. Nestling birds such as robins, nightingales, and mammals such as short-tailed voles and harvest mice are eaten, though mostly these are a minor part of the diet. It is believed by some that dead mammals may occasionally be found and eaten. There are old records of larger grass snakes eating rats, and it is not hard to suppose that a grass snake of over 152 cm (5 feet) could eat much larger prey. Young reptiles often feed upon the young of the adult animals they will eat when they are big enough to subdue them. Young grass snakes will take tadpoles, amphibian metamorphs, earthworms and insects. There are some quite unusual records of grass snakes feeding on honey bees.

The smooth snake's diet may often be exclusively reptilian: they feed upon slow-worms, which can be well over half their size, while sand lizards and common lizards are favourite foods, though all but the largest smooth snakes have difficulty subduing a large adult sand lizard. Young adders and grass snakes are also prey. Cannibalism may occur, though there is little information on this from the wild. Small mammals, particularly nestlings such as pygmy shrews, voles and nightjars and Dartford warbler chicks are also on the menu. Young smooth snakes feed on small reptiles close to their own size; in captivity, they eat slugs, spiders and flies. In the wild

Smooth snake constricting a common lizard.

Lizards will grab at winged insects.

these may be good items to eat when there aren't many larger prey, or when young snakes are still practising their hunting skills. There is also one record of a frog being eaten by a smooth snake.

Adders have the most varied diet of the snakes, feeding on short-tailed field voles as a staple food, in addition to mice, and all species of lizards, nestling birds (including merlin and grouse chicks) and bird's eggs. Toads and other amphibians are also eaten. Earthworms and insects are taken by young adders, as are small lizards and amphibians. It is rumoured that the smooth snake and grass snake are immune to adder venom, but hedgehogs do not have the immunity which folklore suggests (see *Hedgehogs* by Pat Morris in this series).

Sand lizards, like many Lacertids, have the capacity to take food in large amounts when it is available and so take advantage of seasonal abundance. They have good eyesight and actively pursue food until satisfied with quantity; as long as the weather's warm enough, the more there is to eat, the more they will eat. Adult sand lizards have stronger jaws and are able to eat larger, harder-bodied invertebrates than common lizards. The sand lizard diet includes spiders, harvestmen, flies, grasshoppers, beetles, butterflies, moths, hairless caterpillars, weevils, flying ants, earthworms,

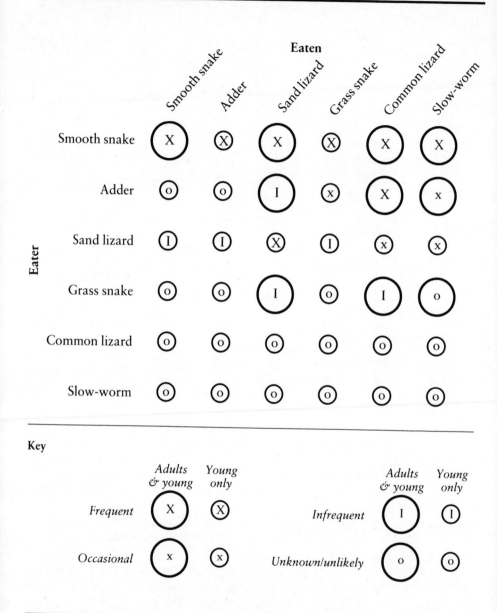

Eaten

Eater ↓ / Eaten →	Smooth snake	Adder	Sand lizard	Grass snake	Common lizard	Slow-worm
Smooth snake	X	(X)	X	(X)	X	X
Adder	o	o	I	x	X	x
Sand lizard	(I)	(I)	(X)	(I)	x	x
Grass snake	o	o	I	o	I	o
Common lizard	o	o	o	o	o	o
Slow-worm	o	o	o	o	o	o

Key

	Adults & young	Young only		Adults & young	Young only
Frequent	X	(X)	Infrequent	I	(I)
Occasional	x	(x)	Unknown/unlikely	o	(o)

Do unto others!

Reptiles have the habit of eating each other and even their own species from time to time. The table shows who eats who, the size of reptile the eater can cope with and how often this is likely to occur.

woodlice, slugs and centipedes. Sand lizards may grab at damsel-flies, bees and hoverflies: in other words they eat most things that are small and not distasteful. This includes young common lizards, slow-worms and even young of their own kind. Cannibalism most often occurs in late autumn when sand lizards hatch out and food for adult lizards is getting scarce. Little is known about why this occurs and how it influences lizard numbers. In captivity this opportunistic feeding may extend to eating discarded scraps of meat and vegetable. There is even a reliable report of a wild sand lizard drinking wild honey from a disturbed bee's nest. ·

Common lizards eat spiders, grasshoppers, harvestmen, craneflies, true bugs, aphids, flies, small beetles, centipedes, earthworms, slugs, flying ants, ant eggs and larvae, bees, wasps, butterflies, moths, caterpillars, and small snails. As with sand lizards, most small invertebrates are fair game. A lizard's diet varies throughout the year as different invertebrates become abundant and then die off.

Slow-worms feed upon slugs, particularly the common slug *Deroceras veticulatum*. Other food includes earthworms, spiders, insects such as ants and their larvae, hairless caterpillars, small snails and rarely the young of other reptiles. It is also possible that slow-worms feed on newly born voles, mice and shrews.

Reptiles may drink from pools, trapped water and other sources of liquid. Lizards drink with the help of their tongues and sometimes sip dew or water droplets on plants. Snakes will submerge the front of their mouths and drink.

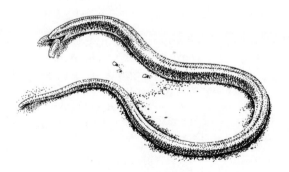

Slug-eating slow-worms are the gardener's friend.

Feeding

Warm weather is required before reptiles really begin to hunt actively and feed. Snakes strike with open mouth at high speed. The smooth snake and grass snake latch on and prevent the prey from escaping, but this is not quite so important for the adder which injects venom, lets go and then after two or three minutes follows the trail of the quickly overpowered prey. Snakes will almost always try to swallow prey head first, and in the case of grass snakes usually alive. Smooth snakes are constrictors, and, following their initial bite, will wrap around their prey with coils, and this serves to constrain the prey before the mouth is slowly edged round to its head. Smooth snakes may anchor their tails to get extra leverage on prey which may be almost the same size as them. Grass snakes often attack in water and may move long distances to a familiar body of water, where they feed on fish or amphibians; adders and smooth snakes will find the best places to wait for or search out lizards. The amount of travelling they must do depends how close are their favourite basking places and overwintering areas.

All three species of snake swallow food whole as a result of the ability of the jaw hinge to dislocate and stretch to allow food through into the gullet and stomach. Small rows of backward pointing teeth grip the prey, while the windpipe protrudes out from the lower inside of the mouth to avoid suffocation during the swallowing process. Copious salivation is required to allow large prey items to slip down easily.

Lizards hunt and grab prey with their mouths, then sometimes shake and stun it and then chomp it around in the mouth a bit before swallowing. The odd cricket or spider leg may be lost in the process, but on the whole the food is swallowed more or less complete. Snakes eat less regularly than lizards and may even go weeks and months without feeding. Frequency of hunting in snakes varies throughout the year, and each species has its own strategy which may differ according to habitat (for example, adders may feed on common lizards in drier places and voles in wetter areas). They may locate prey by sitting and waiting in suitable places, or actively explore or forage.

Snakes may quickly learn which is the most easily available food in their area, and then become familiar with the method of obtaining that diet, sometimes not bothering to search much for other foods. This means that they will sometimes eat what they can clearly recognize, and not pursue scarcer prey. Some populations of snakes can be found in places where prey is limited in variety almost to a single species; some grass snakes, for example, may feed almost exclusively on toads or newts.

Lizards may spend about a quarter of their active time hunting along well known routes that may not be all that productive during much of the year, but they can, if there at the right moment, take advantage of a nest of flying ants swarming. Sand lizards have large stomachs so that they can take advantage of the few occasions each year when food is very abundant. Lizards' diets vary considerably during the year as different species of invertebrate become available. Common lizards are unspecialized insectivores — meaning they eat more or less what is available at any time. They may tackle quite large invertebrates of up to 30 mm (1.2 inches) in length, but faster, stronger species such as wolf spiders can elude them.

Once the breeding season has finished, reptiles can concentrate on feeding, though as females become heavily pregnant their feeding efforts may be reduced. Invertebrate numbers begin to build up towards summer, and young mammals, birds, reptiles and amphibians also become more available. Slow-worms often hunt during the evening especially after rain on warm overcast days. Grass snakes feed heavily in May, and, as previously mentioned, hunt singly and in groups during the evening. I have regularly seen several grass snakes swimming in a warm chalk quarry pond in Kent between 10 p.m. at night and 2 a.m. the next morning. There were a lot of great crested newts in the pond, and the grass snakes were after them, being able to hunt at night because of the unusual warmth of the water.

The lizards and snakes of Britain swallow their food whole.

Snake venom

Snake venoms are varied and complex. Different venoms attack different parts of the body; some attack the nervous system, some the blood, some the body tissues, and some all three at once. Some cause heart failure, others paralysis. Overseas, the World Health Organisation estimates that 30-40,000 people are killed each year by snakes, mostly in Asia, South East Asia, West Africa and tropical America. In Asia the saw-scaled viper is reported to kill 8,000 people annually. The Asian cobra, Russell's viper and fer de lance are other frequent killers. The most lethal land snakes include the Australian desert taipan, Eastern brown snake and Dubois's reef snake. Despite the very toxic bites from some snakes, death can often be prevented by prompt medical treatment. Most deaths occur away from treatment centres. The relative threat from the venom of the dangerous snakes mentioned above makes the adder's bite look relatively weak, but it is wise to treat all snakes with respect. Remember, however, that over eighty per cent of snakes are completely harmless to humans.

Predation

Being a small, thin-skinned, meaty object with a need to lie out in the sun for long periods makes you an attractive meal for a big hungry carnivore. While snakes and lizards do not have the huge numbers of offspring of the amphibians, it is clear that they are important components in the diets of many other species. Young reptiles are little more than tasty scraps for many predators. This probably explains why young reptiles, particularly snakes, are very secretive compared with the adults. Domesticated animals such as cats, dogs, poultry, peacocks and pigs may all 'have-a-go' at adult reptiles as well as young, if sufficiently hungry; human persecution, the greatest influence of all, is in itself an important theme of this book. There are a number of places where snakes are killed by cars in small numbers each year where roads pass through their habitats. One naturalist who studied adders at the turn of the century boiled and ate an adder to determine its taste — 'a combination of fish and flesh'.

Lizards make an easy mouthful, but snakes are more difficult; foxes and wild cats will all tackle them, and snake remains may be found in their burrows or dens. Badgers are also snake predators. Other mammals such as hedgehogs, polecats, rats, weasels, mink and stoats are reptile predators and young adders have even been reported killed by common shrews. Most snakes are probably eaten by birds and these include ospreys, buzzards, harriers, kestrels, hobbies, pheasants, owls, herons, magpies, gulls, crows and ravens. Many other birds may scavenge carrion snakes from kills by others. It has been suggested that the decline in rabbits from myxomatosis has increased the hunting of reptiles by birds of prey.

Lizards are an important source of food to birds like the red-backed shrike.

Lizards provide a smaller, yet more abundant, source of food for predators. Mammal predators feature heavily, and badgers, foxes, hedgehogs and weasels are all likely to hunt them. Snakes, mostly the smooth snake and adder, occasionally grass snakes are significant predators. Birds of prey like eagles, buzzards, kites, harriers, hawks, kestrels and little owls are predators and storks and red backed shrikes have all been watched taking lizards. Juvenile sand lizards and common lizards will be taken by common shrews as well as by smaller birds such as jays, magpies, mistle thrushes, robins and blackbirds, and are typically snatched away from hatching sites as they appear. Even frogs, toads and beetles are reported to occassionally eat young lizards.

Snake-catchers

Witch doctors or healers existed in England when life was short and painful. Survival required homeopathic cures in times before antibiotics. Snake-catchers are referred to in passing in Victorian literature, their main function being to rid areas of unwanted snakes. Their side-line was to use the bodies of snakes to make a grease or linament by separating the fat away from the skin, organs and body of snakes using heat. This was used as medicine, to cure, amongst other things, 'sprains, black eyes, poisoning with brass, bites by rats and horses, rheumatic joints and sore feet in men and dogs'. In the New Forest of Hampshire, in the 17th and 18th centuries adder fat was known as 'a Sovereign balm; 'adder hunters' supplied it to pharmacists of central and western Europe. The last of these, a Mr 'Brusher' Mills, was a charismatic, bearded man who lived in a heather-turf-covered hut near Beaulieu in the New Forest. He carried a hazel stick and tongs to hold snakes; it is reported that his largest bag of snakes (grass snakes, adders and smooth snakes) was one hundred and sixty in one month. As well as making liniment, he also sent snakes to London Zoo, to feed the reptile collection; snake-eating snakes such as cobras required a constant stream of live food. Others continued to collect in the New Forest beyond 1945 for London and Edinburgh Zoos; this drain on our native population no longer continues.

Belief in the medicinal properties of oils and powders made from adders was widespread (but completely unfounded). They were

The fat from snakes was separated by boiling or roasting by snake-catchers and sold as medicine in Europe during the last century.

particularly used in cures for snake bite itself. The fat body was sometimes cut out and tied to a bite or wound, and oil from an adder's liver used to treat bites. In Surrey these remedies were used to treat bitten livestock such as sheep. In Scotland it is reported that a prescribed cure for bites was that a live pigeon should be ripped open and tied to the afflicted area. However, The British Sportsman, or Nobleman, Gentleman and Farmer's Dictionary in 1792 proposed a more culinary response: 'I, garlic, onions, bacon and baysalt all stamped together; II, cover the wound with Venice treacle or mithridate; III, apply, stamped rue, mustard seed, pickled herrings, black soap, deer's suet and bear's grease.' Wrapping a bite with bandages soaked in a lotion from boiled ash tree bark, and rubbing a bite with the head of a dead adder was once apparently widespread, the head being kept in a jar of salt. Snake sloughs were also used as a cure for rheumatism (worn around the knee), for sunstroke and for headache, and it was suggested that a slough should be wrapped round the head for best results. Other cures for adder bite involved drinks consisting of powdered adder.

Defence

As we have seen, basking in the sun can leave you vulnerable to predators, so the ability to rest motionless and camouflaged is very important. There can be no doubt that reptiles are the masters of camouflage and they depend upon this for safety. The pattern on an adder blends beautifully with bracken and dead grass, while grass-snake green blends in well around wetlands. The smooth snake resembles the stems of heather bushes and the slow-worm dry bracken and bramble stems. All have tones and patterns that break up the outline shape of the reptile. Lizard patterns resemble the freckled, dappled surfaces of soil and vegetation, and the skin of all reptiles may change its tones slightly to match their surroundings. In the dunes of Merseyside sand lizards are paler green and match the marram and other plants in which they climb and sit.

Another good tactic is to feign death, and grass snakes may do this when caught, rolling onto their backs, lolling their tongues and going limp. This behaviour is inherited because it reduces injury after capture by a predator and this may allow escape if the predator is distracted or careless for a few seconds with its apparently subdued meal. Other reptiles may alternate passive behaviour with frantic attempts to escape. Grass snakes are reported to have been seen hissing and striking at dogs in an aggressive fashion. Grass snakes tend to void the contents of their lower guts when trapped by a predator or handled by a human, which is a fairly sensible thing to do if you need to slither away at top speed. With this come strong smelling secretions from the anal gland which also may have some role in distracting and deterring predators. Smooth snakes and adders also release such secretions; that of the smooth snake has a slightly bitter smell, while the adder's can be almost musk-like.

Playing dead may assist a grass snake's escape from a careless predator.

Lizards have yet another tactic — the capacity to lose a part or almost all of their tails below the reproductive organs at the base of the tail. This is particularly prone to happen when the tail is pinched. Fracture points in the tail bones give way along places predetermined during bone formation and the spinal cord is capable of rapidly healing over. The process is brought on when, at a given place, eight muscles surrounding the tail bone contract and jettison their attachment to the muscles behind. The shed tail usually twists and convulses for several minutes and may satisfy or at least distract some predators. After a little bleeding, the open tail wound rapidly dries up and begins to heal over. Then new tail growth can begin. It may take several years for a tail to regenerate, and this is a slower process in older animals. Tail tips regenerate better than complete tails. Coloration of 'new' tails is usually a darker, more even colour than the original. Powers of regeneration in slow-worms are not nearly so strong as in the sand and common lizard. The scientific name for slow-worm means brittle snake, and wild slow-worms may readily shed their tails when caught even with careful handling (see 'Reptile watching').

Parasites and diseases

It is difficult to monitor the effect of diseases and parasites in wild reptiles, as you rarely see a sick snake or lizard. A sick snake may seem limp and unwell when handled and may have obvious signs of tumours and infections. In general, few problems are noticed in the wild, while the bringing of reptiles into captivity may leave them vulnerable to other illnesses to which they have never been exposed.

Lizards and snakes certainly have ticks and mites. Mites fasten usually to the eyes, ears, cloaca and the points where limbs join the body. One mite is known as the lizard mite. Sheep ticks are also found on lizards.

The red mite is about the size of a pin head and sucks blood through its host's skin. This mite causes septicemia, and may hide under scales and cause scale abscesses. These may become small hard swellings and scale damage and further infection may follow; the reptile will appear sick. Large numbers of tiny mite larvae may sometimes be found on reptiles.

Parasitic worms such as flatworms, spinyworms, roundworms and tapeworms invade the gut systems of slow-worms, grass snakes, adders and probably other species. Some may be ingested by feeding on amphibians which carry these parasites. These may sometimes be passed on to higher predators such as birds and mammals.

Smaller protozoa and viruses occur, many of which are harmless. Again, not much is documented. Most diseases probably go through cycles; the reptile population may peak and crash, but we have no information on this. Release of any captive animals without screening for disease may create problems. For example released reptiles are suspected of having caused problems in the deserts of California where viral respiratory illness has spread and infected wild tortoise populations.

Fungi are known to infect the nose and nasal passages of hibernating

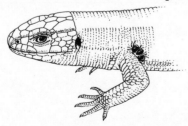

Sheep ticks are found on lizards, often behind a foreleg.

lizards and may attack sand lizard and grass snake eggs. There is one report of a species of dipteran fly parasitizing grass snake eggs.

One of the amazing characteristics of snakes, and one that may in the past have given snakes a supernatural image, is their amazing power of recovery from wounding. Though reptiles do not have strong powers of re-growth of limbs or digits (apart from lizards' tails), localized tissue growth and a strong resistance to some infections enables eventual recovery from huge injuries. Snakes found cut by lawn mowers or stabbed by garden forks, and chewed up slow-worms brought in by the cat have effected full recoveries. I recently looked after an adder which was found on a country lane in Suffolk with a badly damaged head. One eye was pushed in and distorted, and the skull and jaw all but crushed. It looked as if the head had been run over by a car or motor cycle. Within three weeks the eye, jaw and skull had regained a normal, if slightly distorted, appearance, and full alertness was restored. The snake was released near to where it was found, and I hope we will see it again some day to fully document its recovery.

Other malformations of the types found in most animals and plants may occur in snakes and lizards, but these individuals seldom survive for long. Scars from tumours and infections may be found in wild specimens and are most noticeable on the lighter underside of snakes. Some scars are slight, such as those incurred by female reptiles during mating. Unsuccessful attack from predators may also result in scars and injury. Freshly killed and injured reptiles are occasionally found where dropped or discarded. The sloughing of skins assists new scale tissue to form and heal over injuries, until they are eventually repaired. Scars can often be a useful way of recognizing individual reptiles from year to year when trying to observe them in the wild.

Uses and abuses of snakes

The varied acts of snake dancers are still popular in Britain.

Attitudes towards animals are reinforced by the media. Sadly, articles in the press on extreme behaviour towards snakes tend to perpetuate the prejudices against them. While we need to beware of being over-sensitive to 'animalist' attitudes, the British press has a pretty poor track record in their reporting on snake matters, and a flick through the newspaper cuttings file is a real eye-opener.

Most local newspapers are, thankfully, gradually moving away from silly stories about snakes. These are often simply a focus of interest for journalists to write about local people. Keepers of reptiles are portrayed as slightly weird (they often clearly are), and the occasional celebrity, tattooed strongman or publican uses large pythons or boas to attract attention. The captions read 'Snakes Alive', 'Hissing Sid', or other variations on a joky-scare. 'Exotic snake on the loose' is another type of story which fills spaces between the advertising, as snakes are supreme escapologists.

Stories are also frequently written about the boas and pythons used by performing artistes — usually dancers, pin-up models and strippers. There is an emphasis on the erotic associations of snakes.

Publicity also arises when someone sees a snake or slow-worm on a path, bank or at a beauty spot. More than one will probably result in a 'plague of snakes' being reported. An 'adder alert' goes out, and local policemen, scouts, prominent persons in the local community and even Members of Parliament are often proud to announce their saving of the local people from the 'lurking menace at number 32'. The story is quickly dropped when a local naturalist identifies the mangled corpses as slow-worms or grass snakes.

In recent years public attention towards environmental problems has increased. There has been more in-depth reporting on reptile issues. Stories on habitat destruction and endangered species being smuggled through airports are more commonplace. Reptiles are increasingly being used by advertising agencies as symbols of mystery, beauty and strength. Regrettably, their use on television as symbols of fear undoes a lot of hard campaigning to improve the image of snakes.

Snakes and lizards will probably always retain a strong public interest and we need to kindle favourable associations with them in order to break down unfounded prejudices. This is the only way they will be valued in the long term and remain a part of our wildlife.

Reptile watching

Knowing why reptiles are likely to be out in the open is the key to finding and watching them. But the initial decision of where to go and locate reptiles is not easy for the beginner, and, like learning about most secretive or rare animals, it is best to ask someone who has gained experience if you can join them on an outing, even if at first you may need to travel some way to do so. You should be prepared to give up as much time as will be needed, and not to be put off by a day without sightings, though these should be rare once you get your eye in.

The weather is a big determining factor of reptile activity at any time of year — particularly the pattern of each day's sunshine and changes in air temperature. If warm enough, reptiles may be active after just a short burst of sun. Wind activity may also play an important role, as north or east winds may chill exposed open habitats. As long as it is not too hot, calm, cloudless conditions are often best. A short rainy period followed by sun is one of the best times to see reptiles. Wet, warm ground makes their movement easier and reduces the risks of being caught away from a favoured resting place. An individual will have some time to explore before the next dry period, which might perhaps be a drought and enforce summer dormancy (aestivation) in a less suitable refuge.

Hot days in spring after a rainstorm can be very good for watching reptiles. The ground almost seems to steam and the earth, heather and gorse

have a strong distinctive smell. Sunny days with patchy cloud can also be very good, especially cooler days, when reptiles will scuttle in and out of refuges as the sun goes in and out, and this might last all day. On a very hot, sunny day reptiles may give up basking after a few hours in the morning and all you get is sunburn. I have found reptiles on warm but sunless days and evenings when they have been sitting under bits of metal or other debris which are cold, probably in the hope of warmth to come. I have even found them on sunny days sitting out or moving in bursts of light rain. There are occasional exceptions to the general rule, but you will get to recognize favourable conditions. After a while, it will be enough just to stick your head out of the bedroom window a little after sunrise to sense the elements, and you will know if it is going to be a good day to watch reptiles in your area. This is also true during the day when you may be able to judge where reptiles will be most active on slopes facing different directions or with different levels of tree shade. When a cloudy front moves across your county you may play the game of chasing the sun, watching reptiles where the sun decides to shine.

Once you have arrived at the area to be surveyed, your strategy depends to a large extent on how much time you have and how big is the area you wish to cover. In a large area, it may be best to walk briskly but carefully, scanning the ground a few metres ahead for likely basking places in order to familiarize yourself with the area. Remember that noise, ground vibrations and shadow will make reptiles scuttle away. Walking into the sun reduces the clarity of your vision when looking amongst vegetation. It is best to angle your approach so that your shadow falls in front of you but away from the area you are scanning. Reptiles, especially adders, have a good sense of smell, so if possible approach into the wind. Following these guidelines will at first enable you to cover the ground quickly, and see a few glimpses of reptiles before they startle away. With a little practice you will begin to see some reptiles before they see or smell you. It may take several visits before you find a small population of reptiles, so be patient and visit the same spot several times. Some people like to use binoculars to scan ahead for reptiles. Good basking places are often sheltered spots between shrubs. Familiarize yourself with pictures of each reptile so you know the patterns that will help you to decide which species and sexes you have seen. Once you know an area well, repeat visits can be carried out more carefully, and a slow, stealthy approach will help you see more individuals. Look for the tell-tale patterns deep in vegetation. The occasional rustle may be heard, perhaps deep in a grassy tussock. Even these will become familiar, and you will detect the sand lizard's heavy rustle as opposed to the lighter one of the common lizard; the longer rustling of snakes will become very recognizable. Lizards and snakes will often return after a short while to the point from which you disturbed them. You should not dive into or disturb vegetation, it is better to return after about ten minutes. Snakes may disappear for longer periods before returning to the same spot. Looking under discarded rubbish for reptiles and their sloughs (see Sloughing) can be fruitful, particularly when the weather turns poor after a bright start to the day.

Some researchers have used radio-tracking in order to follow patterns of movement in reptiles. A small transmitter may be attached to lizards by a harness, or in snakes force-fed into the gut or surgically implanted in the body cavity through a small incision. This is no doubt inconvenient and uncomfortable for the individuals and must influence behaviour. While snakes have a capacity to survive implants, studies show that these methods may expose animals to stress and risk of infection, and can leave them more vulnerable to predators.

The best information is often gained at first hand, simply by putting in enough time. Without spending time in the field you will never see reptiles contesting, fighting, feeding, breeding and giving birth where they belong, in the wild. I have never had a disappointing day. As with fishing, your quiet stealthy methods will bring many animals and plants to your attention. A day's highlight may be finding a patch of orchids in full flower or watching a stretch of unspoiled heathland as a fiery sunset fills the sky and falls behind windswept pines.

Handle with care

Unless you are taking part in an organized study, it is best not to handle wild reptiles. Often more information can be gained simply by quietly watching reptiles rather than trying to catch them. The smooth snake and sand lizard are protected under the Wildlife and Countryside Act (1981). To handle smooth snakes and sand lizards you will require a special licence from the Nature Conservancy Council. This is because, like birds, reptiles can be easily damaged by incorrect handling, and because these two species are considered so rare in Britain even photographing them requires a special permission from the NCC.

Handling reptiles is a skill of its own, and the techniques require practice, confidence and care. It will probably not be long before training will be a requisite for those involved in surveys that require repeated handling, much as bird ringers are given a training before they start handling birds.

Techniques of handling differ with each species. The smooth snake is the quietest, most passive snake, rarely making much effort to escape and only occasionally biting when handled. It is best to wear clean, thin but strong gloves when handling snakes, and to avoid being bitten — not only, obviously, for your own sake, but because snakes can damage their teeth and mouths quite easily and this can lead to infections. Gloves will also protect you from accidental bites from adders, which you may not see lying hidden and close to other harmless species. Melanistic (black) and albino (colourless) reptiles occur from time to time and with occasional colour variations in snakes it is better to be safe than sorry should you mistake an individual snake. While gloves may be uncomfortable to wear, they are essential for serious studies when adders may be present and where you must examine as many individuals as possible. It is best to hold smooth snakes and grass snakes with both hands to avoid straining their muscles and backbones; do not hold them by the tail tip. Grass snakes disappear like lightning when they see you, so you must stalk them, trying to get a glimpse before you dive and gently grab them. The other way is to locate them and then manoeuvre yourself so that you are in the line of their approach when you can then quickly catch them as they twine through vegetation (I once had a grass snake anchor onto a leg of my waders in the middle of a pond!). They will usually thrash around when caught, flicking faeces and strong smelling secretions from the anal gland over you. Adders and smooth snakes may do this to a lesser extent (see Defence).

Adders when caught may hiss and strike. Firm but gentle handling and no pinching or squeezing, will, with practice, put many snakes and lizards quite at ease. This can be achieved by very gradually reducing grip to the minimum required on their supported bodies to prevent them from escaping.

Catching adders should NOT be attempted without expert guidance, and requires special care not to damage the snake or get yourself bitten. Adders and all British snakes should NOT be pinned down with a stick or foot, as bruising to the throat or body may occur and this could prevent feeding for weeks. The windpipe, ribs and internal organs could also be damaged by crushing. With pregnant snakes pinning or rough handling may damage the developing young, causing stillbirth. You should also be careful to avoid handling snakes that have just eaten as they are likely to disgorge their meal at you. Since the snake will have spent time and energy finding its food, this may be a serious setback for it. One technique for catching adders is to locate them with stealth and then move quickly within easy reach. Adders will often flush (startle) relatively slowly and seek to lock their heads into adjacent vegetation to pull themselves more quickly away. In doing this they straighten out and it is usually quite simple to restrain the tail end with your gloved fingers to prevent escape. Adders, like humans, have variable temperaments, according both to the individual and to how hot and bothered they are. Usually it is quite easy to gently free the body from vegetation and restrain the snake for examination. Adders may be restrained for examination in clear plastic tubing of the correct diameter. Putting dots of non-toxic coloured paint on individuals may assist with re-identification — but only until they next slough their skins. But remember, never handle reptiles unless you absolutely have to.

Like snakes, lizards can move quite fast and also do not like to be pinched, which can lead to the shedding of tails. Jettisoning a tail is an expensive loss of energy to a lizard. The slow-worm, sand lizard and common lizard should never be held or caught by their tails. Stalking lizards and then pouncing with a cupped hand is very hit and miss and chancy in terms of both catching the individual and risking its tail. Noosing is the preferred method for serious fieldworkers. This method again requires special training and involves the use of a special noose made from fishing twine on the end of a thin flexible pole about 2 metres long. Lizards will often realize you are present but not startle away until you come too close. From a distance they will examine a noose, not realizing it is a trap, and often lift their heads to examine it as you gently manoeuvre it into place. Once over the neck, a quick tug secures the slip knot and the lizard is lifted swiftly into your free hand. This is a tricky technique. Lizards should be held with the thumb

and first two fingers by the upper body and shoulders. The rest of the body is held between the bent palm and last two fingers. Handling is not really required for most purposes; remember to act always within the law.

Keeping records of your findings is very important, and a notebook is advisable. At the end of a year it is quite useful to write up your research and present it to your Parish or District Council with any recommendations

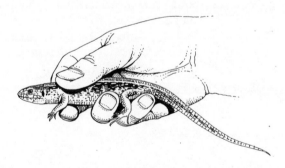

Reptiles must be held gently but firmly to avoid their injury or escape.

you may wish them to take up to protect or enhance reptile habitats in your area. Your local natural history society and county naturalists trust may also be interested.

It is always a good idea to contact local records centres, naturalists' societies, or other conservation groups to swap information and plan the most interesting searches. Your results may eventually become part of regional or national recording schemes, which help to determine trends in changing status of reptiles.

Photographs are often the best way to record your findings, and you can get definite confirmation of your identifications. For more detailed studies, record cards can be kept, listing length and identifying features of individuals. Sloughs can be taken home for careful examination and stored for future comparison. It is worth noting weather conditions and positions of your finds in order to build up a picture of why and how reptiles are living on your particular site. Recording body markings so that individuals can be identified after a year or longer is of clear interest to population studies. Ventral scale clipping in snakes and toe clipping in lizards are often carried out in scientific studies but should not be attempted without prior training from an expert, and you will need a permit. Discoloration of ventral scales from scale clipping will rarely last longer than six years, often less. Body pattern recording is now more often chosen as the preferred method. Recording the position and nature of body scars is often a useful way to identify individuals, and ventral scale counts are also useful.

Sexing snakes can be quite tricky; males usually have a proportionally longer tail than females; the male testis are positioned in the base of the tail behind the vent. The table gives a guide to sexing snakes from counting sub-caudal (between vent and tail tip) scales, though there are some overlaps. It is worth here saying a bit about scale arrangements. The underside of snakes has a single row of broad scales called ventral scales. The scale covering the vent is slightly larger and called the anal scale and is usually divided into two halves. Behind the vent, scales are divided into two rows of sub-caudal scales which get smaller and smaller down to a single terminal spine at the tail tip which we do not count.

	females	borderline	males
Grass snakes	49 to 61	61/62	63 to 73
Smooth snakes	44 to 52	53/54	55 to 62
Adders	22 to 32	33/38	39 to 46

Sub-caudal scale counts for male and female snakes, giving approximate range of variation within sexes and the approximate borderline where numbers of scales alone is not a good indication of sex.

Snake bite

Adders are the only snakes in Britain capable of harmful bites to humans. While the smooth snake has tiny vestigial venom glands at the back of the mouth which produce a neurotoxin, these are sufficiently small to be redundant. Adders have two methods of attack: one is a jabbing action, where contact is only made for a fraction of a second, and might best be described as a 'sting'. A fuller bite to a prey animal, or perhaps the finger or toe of a luckless human, involves the lower jaw more intimately in the action of biting. On contact, pressure from the bitten object causes venom to flow out to the fangs from a pair of venom glands lying along the side of the adder's head behind the eye. Snake fangs are made from dentine, folded to channel venom to its tip. The fang is fixed like the head of a dart to an especially short maxilla bone (see diagram), and this in turn joins to the skull. When a snake strikes, muscles pull the maxilla bone and fang forward, out from a protective fleshy sheath. Fangs are easily displaced and are replaced by a chain of developing reserve fangs every so often and as frequently as every six weeks in summer. Fully grown, the fangs are up to 7mm in length. The defensive 'stab or strike range' of an adder is only up to about 15cm. Adder venom is a viscous pale amber liquid of enzymes and other proteins, and a few drops (as little as 0.01ml) is all that may be required to kill a small lizard in a few seconds.

The risks from adders to humans, pets and livestock are not severe. A full adder bite may impart less than half the amount of venom thought to

In a feeding bite by an adder, venom flows forward from the paired glands in the head into the body of the prey.

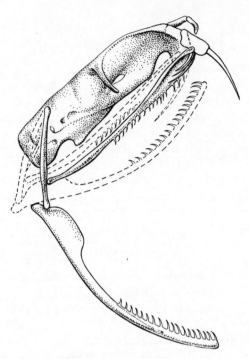

An adder's skull, showing the position at rest (dotted) and with the fangs pulled forward during a bite.

put humans at real risk. Most people are bitten when trying to catch or kill adders, usually during recreation or when on holiday. Dogs are often bitten, particularly gun dogs, which search with their heads close to the ground. Bites are most frequent in spring and autumn when adders are caught unaware during their pre- or post-hibernation lying-out periods by careless picnickers and their dogs. Walkers, ramblers and climbers should watch where they sit, walk or climb in heathy or rocky ground. Obviously bare feet leave the walker exposed, and young children and dogs should be kept close at hand on warm or sunny days when moving through land which could be snake habitat.

The effect of adder bite on livestock — cows, horses, ponies, sheep and goats — rarely ends in death. A year-long survey of veterinary practices in south Dorset reported that of 33 domestic animals bitten (22 dogs, 7 cats, 3 cows and 1 goat) no cases proved fatal, even though some were bitten on the nose and jaw. Dogs bitten on a paw may take three weeks before they are walking normally and often animals will seem severely debilitated prior to full recovery.

An investigation of published information on human adder bite victims during the period 1876-1976 revealed only 14 human deaths, spread more or less evenly over the decades. Eight of the victims were either under the age of 12 or over 50 years old, but this may not necessarily reflect a vulnerability in these age ranges. It is interesting that there are not more deaths reported from the last century, when the rural labour force approached 2 million people and the early part of this century, when rural land management was less mechanized, and human-snake contact more likely. Thomas Bell, who wrote on adders in 1848, did not mention any fatal bites from adders. A death from adder bite would surely have been made widely known. One answer might be that with a smaller, fragmented population people were more in tune with their surroundings and understood how to avoid snake bite. This seems possible but unlikely because a proportion of bites are accidental. My conclusion is that fatality from adder bite in the UK has always been a very rare event. Small farm animals and dogs are more regularly bitten, and almost all recover. Deaths of pets and livestock from adder bite are very hard to find. There are, however a few older reports of adder bite being made worse by vets injecting anti-venom. Even bites to the muzzle and head of dogs are commonly survived, though they may very rarely cause blindness in one eye or deafness in one ear. With

humans, the death rate suggests that about one person in a decade of bites has died in Britain, and with perhaps one hundred bites each year, the fatal risk must be about one in a thousand bites. The probability of being killed by a snake in Britain is far less than the probability of being killed by a bee, or dog or in a horse accident.

Human death from adder bite results from allergic reaction to adder venom, causing shock and heart failure in a minority of people who might have a more sensitive immune system. Such persons might be equally vunerable to bee, wasp or insect stings which in Britain kill about sixty people each decade. Cardiac failure in humans following adder bite is reported to cause death between 6 and 60 hours following a bite.

Symptoms

Adder venom is haematoxic, attacking the blood system; haemorrhaging and blood coagulation may occur. The bite itself may be painless or resemble a light prick from a bramble. If venom has been injected, the bitten limb begins to swell and ache often within the first few minutes. This usually increases, with a further spread of swelling. After about half an hour, symptoms may include stomach cramps, and aching in the small of the back. There may be tenderness of glands under the arm and groin and an increase in body temperature. Shivering and shaking, sweating, giddiness, diarrhoea, dryness in the mouth and feeling nauseous are all unpleasant symptoms to anticipate once bitten. The body clearly has to respond to internal pollution and the amount of venom injected by a bite may vary considerably. Discoloration of the bitten limb or area is usual, and spectacular colours more familiar in bruising are often seen, sometimes with blistering of skin around the bite. Thirst, loss of appetite and dehydration may occur. Hospital treatment is needed for those perhaps with less immunity who may move from drowsiness and unco-ordinated movement into temporary loss of consciousness, and difficulty with breathing and swallowing. The peak effects seem to take place between 6 and 48 hours. Most recoveries take from one to two weeks. Under medical supervision, tests for allergic response to the available treatments will first be carried out. Antibiotics, antihistamines and anti-tetanus injections will all help. To reduce the effect of blood coagulation within the body, transfusion of a few pints of plasma may aid recovery. An anti-venom injection to help destroy toxins may be quite small, and often not even required at all if stable improvement persists.

Anti-venom

From about 1936 until 1964, the Pasteur Institute in France produced what was known as ER Antiviperin (for use as an antidote to all snake bites)

First aid for adder bites

1. Stay calm and do not run. There is a good chance that the snake is not venomous or, if venomous, it has not injected much venom.

2. Do not attempt to kill or capture the snake.

3. Do not cut the wound or attach a tourniquet.

4. Sit quietly. As soon as swelling begins, go calmly to the nearest point of human contact or telephone and report the event to someone who can assist you for the next few hours. Rest the bitten area as much as possible. Do not do anything to increase your rate of heart beat.

5. If swelling spreads more than a few inches from the bite and you start to feel unwell, ask to be taken to your nearest medical centre or hospital casualty department. You will probably be transferred to a place with better monitoring and treatment facilities.

The usual effect of an adder bite to the hand is a swelling of the hand and arm and discomfort for a day or so.

mainly from culturing antibodies in the blood systems of horses. This is achieved by injecting small amounts of venom into horses and then collecting and removing the antibodies from the lymph system. The venom of North African snakes was most frequently used. As more cases of snake bite and treatment were studied improved legislation such as the Therapeutic Substances Act 1956 started to improve the standards for treatment of venomous snake bite. Europe in the 1960s saw human population expansion into neglected or undisturbed land, and this was bringing people into contact with European vipers such as asps and nose-horned vipers; some less, some more dangerous than the adder. In 1961, for example, one manufacturer of anti-venom in Europe reported around four hundred requests for anti-venom to treat snake bite. The unpurified horse serum being supplied was suspected, however, of causing protein or anaphylactic shock and subsequent heart failure, and while it may have saved lives its use may also have been responsible for the suffering or even death of both humans and livestock treated. A German company Behringwerke AG developed a more refined anti-venom, and in a period of just a few decades, medical science had advanced from the rubbing-in of potassium permanganate (which reassured victims at the cost of causing aggravated sores) to an advanced technique which today saves the lives of those bitten by more highly venomous snakes around the world.

'Thou art cursed'

When the devil, disguised as a serpent, tempted Eve with a heavenly apple, it was a bad press-day for reptiles. A flick through the Bible confirms the longstanding public profile of

snakes as untrustworthy and evil: 'thou art cursed above all cattle, above every beast of the field; upon thy belly shalt thou go, and dust shalt thou eat all the days of thy life...' Like a good tale, in one form or another, it swept the Judaeo Christian world, and boomed from pulpit and bookshelves around the world. But, like most frame-ups, the truth is now coming out. Even to the Greeks and Romans, the Aesculapian snake was a symbol of healing. Reptiles may have been used for charms or cures, but they were also fair game for 'the pot', as they still are around much of the world today.

Victorian Britain saw agricultural workers suffering from low wages and a low standard of living. The rosy ideal of rural living portrayed so vividly and romantically by painters was being shattered. In Wild Life in a Southern County by Richard Jefferies we gain an insight into the attitudes of rural labourers in southern England, in this case gangs of hay cutters and stackers, harvesting by hand vast acres of hay:

When the mowers have laid the tall grass in swathes snakes are often found on them or under them by the haymakers, whose prongs or forks throw the grass about to expose a large surface to the sun. The haymakers kill them without mercy, and numbers thus meet with their fate. The mowers who sleep a good deal under the hedges have a tradition that a snake will sometimes crawl down a man's throat if he sleeps on the ground with his mouth open. (These snakes are) . . . bred in the stomachs of human beings, from drinking out of ponds and streams frequented by water snakes . . . such snakes (have) . . . been vomited by the unfortunate persons afflicted with this strange calamity.

Even taxonomists working in the eighteenth century to catalogue animals and plants seemed dubious about reptilian credentials. The famous taxonomist Linnaeus, in his summary of reptiles and amphibians in Systema Naturae, begins his review with the words 'These foul and loathsome animals . . .'! He described most of the British reptiles in 1758 from specimens caught in Switzerland and Sweden; he must in some instances have been pushed for time as he lumped two species, the common and sand lizards, as one species, despite their probable abundance in places he would have visited at that time. In the next century Thomas Bell's early book History of British Reptiles *was one of the earliest comprehensive descriptions of British reptiles. He lived in Poole in Dorset but strangely never saw a smooth snake in the vast heathlands surrounding the area at that time. Irrespective of learned goings-on in towns, rural communities* continue to this day the traditional image of snakes as the devil incarnate, as in this North Country litany:

> From witches and wizards
> asps, efts and lizards
> and creeping things that run in
> hedge bottoms,
> Good Lord deliver us.

A nation of animal lovers?

How do we really value our native wildlife compared with our 'creature-comforts'? An examination of the records of deaths involving animals in the UK during 1983 revealed that in that year 44 people died as a result of animal-related causes. In 1983 no one was killed by an adder, but 6 adults were killed by bee and insect stings, horses were involved in 33 deaths and dog bites killed 2. Dog bites kill humans relatively frequently and in England and Wales each year there are about 214,000 dog-associated injuries receiving hospital treatment, of which about 209,000 (97.7%) are bites, costing the National Health Service an estimated £7 million per year. Non-medical costs of dog accidents are estimated as exceeding £40 million per year. In other words we spend almost as much repairing the damage from this one species in the UK than is allocated from our taxes towards the entire annual budget of the government conservation body — the Nature Conservancy Council. In financial terms we have valued our pets far more than our declining wild animals and plants.

The killing has to stop

Why Britain's snakes are not slippery customers

They're not adders, says Ted

moment of fear

Fight to save snakes

Snakes alive

Learn to love thy snake

When snakes make your skin crawl

NO-ONE WANTS HISSING SID

Torture shock over reptiles

Fergie's

'Save our snakes'

Call to save snakes from torture

SNAKE ALIVE!

Snakes alive! Keep 'em that way

Snakes in the grass

Anyone with an open sunny garden may, cats permitting, be lucky enough to have a resident reptile or two. Reptiles can be encouraged in gardens, much as they can be in wildlife reserves, and the guidelines for gardener and reserve manager are quite similar. Reptiles need basking places that are undisturbed by both people and pets. It is easy to see why large gardens are needed; going within a few metres of reptiles, if repeated several times, will almost always scare them away. Completely neglected gardens (but with the exception of habitat management to prevent overgrowing) are best for reptiles. Gardens situated in a sunny position are good as they offer more sunlight, and will heat up the small wind-shaded patches of short grass, lichens, moss or bare soil favoured by reptiles. Try and encourage heathy plants such as grasses, heather, gorse and small trimmed hedge-plants on sheltered south-facing banks.

Good feeding sites for lizards, with plenty of invertebrates, can be encouraged with wood stacks and compost heaps. Garden ponds can also be beneficial as they enable amphibian populations to establish. Small clumps of ground with rushes within flooded grassland are used by grass snakes and adders when they hunt. Dry refuge and overwintering sites used by reptiles include dry-stone walls, rockeries or other piles of stones and wood. Those covered with topsoil are often most suitable.

Many of our towns and cities border what is often called green belt, where reptile populations may be able to take temporary advantage of neglected garden 'wastelands' and fragments of untouched habitats. These may attract reptiles by reason of features such as rubbish dumps, which may have a higher density of food. Walled gardens may be invaded for their value as artificial sun traps and some gardeners deliberately introduce slow-worms for their slug-eating capacity.

Grass snakes, which range widely, may enter farms, large estates, and also quite small gardens to feed, sun themselves and breed. Feeding on goldfish and frogs, toads, newts and tadpoles is commonly reported. Often the grass snake is castigated for doing so even though it is performing an important predatory regulation of pond life. Fish keepers may, however, not appreciate this when they find an expensive little fish has become a snack; little can be done except to tightly cover a pond with fine netting. This seems a shame and it often interferes with plant life. Perhaps it is better to relax in a deckchair and feel good about your contribution to saving

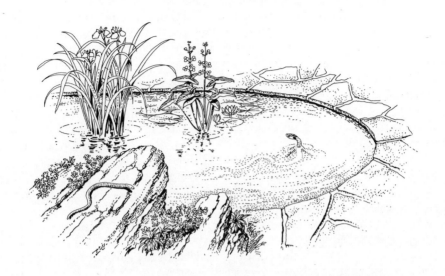

part of our natural environment. Stronger, more alert goldfish may survive to be too big for a grass snake to handle. Garden ponds are good in general for many types of wildlife and should be encouraged. Guidance on creating, or, better still, restoring old ponds in your neighbourhood can be found in a number of recent publications on this subject. It may be worth having one pond for things like fish breeding, and one left completely for wildlife: the two can be merged only with very careful pond design, diligent management and patience.

Reptiles can occasionally be found in well established rockeries of quite small gardens. I recently found a small community of the four commoner British reptiles in the gardens of a row of terraced houses, centred on one which had been left neglected. When the neglected one was disturbed for redevelopment, the reptiles were removed, and over fifty slow-worms, ten adders, a handful of grass snakes and common lizards were quickly caught and released back to the wild at a safer site nearby. Many appeared to be permanent residents though it was clear that a larger area was being used by some. A reptile breeding in a garden may go under next door's shed to hibernate, and over the back fence to find frogs or fish in an adjoining pond. If your garden backs onto a railway line, canal bank, hedgerow or other suitable habitat, visiting reptiles may pop in from time to time. It is not unusual for me to be called out to identify reptiles in such circumstances; often slow-worms are being mistaken for adders. In most cases reptiles present no problem at all, all that is needed is an explanation to those concerned of the reason for snakes or lizards being present, and how to treat snakes with caution and identify them. My young niece had no prejudices about the hatchling grass snakes I showed her; she had a gentle 'touch' without prompting, and I do not believe that humans are born with any instinctive fear of snakes. However, it can be hard to tell a one-year-old baby sitting on the lawn not to play with a passing adder, and so caution and sensible action is necessary. (Pigs were once used to remove snakes from areas near houses, particularly rattlesnakes from parts of the USA.)

There are old beliefs in Britain which may hold some truth that snakes are sensitive to strong smells and will avoid smoke. ('Burning hartshorn, lily root, ash tree boughs, or old shoes'!) It has also been suggested that snakes can be discouraged by 'planting wormwood' or 'by placing a well beaten mixture of onions and river crabfish.' There is also an old report of an Irishman importing native soil to his new home in Australia in an attempt to bring the influence of St Patrick to his garden! If adders do on the rare occasion reach nuisance levels, or more likely you just want advice and to know what reptiles you may have seen, it is best to put the matter into the hands of an expert. A visit on a sunny day will usually put your mind at rest and enable you to watch and enjoy them and show others. Certainly *never* try to kill any reptile, as you could hurt yourself and are likely to be breaking the law.

Dung heaps

Grass snakes can be found in. gardens, where they use compost heaps as egg laying sites. Compost gardeners, who ferment their grass, leaves and other organic matter into natural fertilizer will know all about this. Huge steaming heaps can be made with fiery insides caused by micro-organisms breaking down plant matter. Mushroom farmers, stable and cow-shed muckers and those who empty the lawn mower may all have noticed clusters of white grass snake's eggs when turning natural refuse heaps in autumn. The eggs are hidden below the surface, gently warming. Eggs have also been found in quite small, tidy compost heaps and anyone with a passing grass snake may help to boost numbers by preparing a suitable nesting heap. The trick to a good compost heap is to raise it above the ground with wooden

Reptiles may visit gardens for food, shelter and quiet basking places.

shuttering to allow air to enter underneath. The stack should be as big as possible. Do not add fibrous material or sticks, or anything that may not break down fairly easily. Grass clippings are really the best of all because of their large surface area, but I have seen grass snake eggs in mixed compost heaps containing all sorts of things, including potato peelings. Grass snakes will look for breeding sites early in the summer and so prepare your pile of grass cuttings, manure or sawdust as early as possible in the year. It may take a year for the snakes to find it and a second year to begin to start using it for egg laying. If necessary, in June, turn it carefully to improve the evenness of decomposition before egg-laying. Apart from seeing grass snakes on your heap, small tell-tale holes may be found as the snakes create tunnels within the heap.

Snakestones

Snakestones, or serpent stones, are pieces of smooth, rounded stone, allegedly of mystical origin, but probably unusual river-ground pebbles, or carved stones from ancient burial mounds. They were believed to have special properties: they were once in common use in Britain and other countries. Snake or adder stones were used for a number of purposes, including as ingredients for drinks to cure adder bites. More usually, they were attached to the puncture mark or incisions around an adder bite and then soaked in milk to release the venom said to have been absorbed by the stone. In Borlase's Antiquities of Cornwall it is reported that:

Snakestones are thought to have been taken from rivers and ancient burial mounds in Britain, or to have originated overseas.

'The country people have a persuasion that the snakes here breathing upon a hazel wand produce a stone ring of blue colour in which there appears the yellow figure of a snake, and that beasts bit and envenomed being given some water to drink wherein this stone has been infused, will perfectly recover of the poison . . . in most parts of Wales and throughout all Scotland, and in Cornwall, we find it a common opinion of the vulgar that about Midsummer-eve (though in the time they do not all agree) it is usual for snakes to meet in companies, and that by joining heads together and hissing, a kind of bubble is formed, which the rest, by continual hissing, blow on till it passes quite through the body, and then it immediately hardens and resembles a glass ring, which whoever finds shall prosper in all his undertakings'.

There are stories from Glamorgan that a snake would kill another snake and then weave a ball on its tail which would bring prosperity to the finder.

There are several other local superstitions about the adder: some can be easily explained, others remain a mystery. In Devon, for example, it was believed that if a cow was bitten by an adder, the shape of the adder would be reproduced in the cream at the next milking. In Newcastle and parts of Wales it was thought that a spider crawling over the back of an adder would cause it to be rendered harmless. In Lincolnshire it was said that adders spat poison into the air at larks, killing them stone dead and causing them to fall and be eaten. Adders are no longer believed to swallow their young to protect them when they are threatened. There is a report that when people believed female adders were killed by the act of giving birth, that anyone killing a parent risked being drowned in a bag with an adder as punishment.

Trade

Since 1981 it has been illegal to sell any of the British reptiles without a licence from the Department of the Environment. Offenders face fines, particularly for interfering with smooth snakes and sand lizards. However, dealers and pet shops are still given licences to sell our commoner native reptiles, a situation which surely must soon change; they may take a toll on isolated populations where little is known about the effect of removing them. An area like Tyne and Wear is a good example; only one or two grass snake sites remain. In 1983 I found a market stall in central Newcastle where illegally locally collected grass snakes were for sale. Pet shops may buy reptiles for a small amount from local children who catch them in the small pockets of rough land in urban areas. This situation does little to kindle responsible attitudes in children towards wildlife.

A paradox in the laws protecting British reptiles is that it is often legal to remove 'commoner' reptiles from Sites of Special Scientific Interest — which are supposed to be some of the most protected areas for nature conservation in the country. Even though they might be vital food for smooth snakes or other rare animals, it would be perfectly legal, with a

land-owner's permission, to remove slow-worms and common lizards from an SSSI.

Confusion arises over importing of species found in Britain from overseas. International Conventions and European Community legislation has helped reduce some of the mass importation of reptiles entering the UK and with luck it will not be long before all speculative pet trade in wild reptiles is. banned. Many imported reptiles die during or within a few months of importation, and are frequently passed on to the general public when sick, underfed and dehydrated. The main market for small reptiles is the novelty pet trade. A small number of reckless dealers and keepers dirty the image of legitimate captive breeding and have hindered professionalism.

European and other exotic reptiles imported into the UK are usually dead within a very short space of time, partly because they are transported incorrectly. They may suffer extremes of heat or chilling, be subjected to stress, filthy bags or containers or be crammed together too tightly. I have often seen at first hand, and been told of, disgusting conditions of shipments arriving at airports and in temporary holding at houses of 'private dealers'. In recent years the mass importation of reptiles for captivity has become a considerable cause for concern and the trade in pet tortoises, for example, has been exposed. Trade controls have stimulated some responsible keeping and breeding of tortoises, but regrettably lessons have not yet been learned with regard to snakes and lizards.

Reptiles and the law

There are a number of Acts of Parliaments relating to British reptiles. You must pick your way through the legal jargon to appreciate the values, the faults and the ambiguities in our laws. Anyone really serious about understanding legislation can get copies of the Acts from those bookshops that stock HMSO publications. The following is a brief summary of these.

The Wildlife and Countryside Act 1981 was designed to protect wildlife, including the smooth snake and sand lizard, by making it illegal to harm them directly or to damage their habitats. The Act is considered as the legal instrument to implement the Bern Convention on the Conservation of European Wildlife and Natural Habitats, and should soon be fully implemented when Britain reinforces measures as part of the efforts of the European Community to protect wildlife within Europe. The 1981 Act makes it an offence to do the following to the smooth snake and sand lizard:

– Intentionally kill or injure them or have in possesion or control any live or dead or any part of them.

– Disturb, damage or destroy any place used for shelter or protection.

– Sell, offer, hold for sale or advertise for them, live or dead.

— Kill them without 'reasonable avoidance' when given permission to destroy their habitats by legalisation that supersedes the Act.

The last category is a loophole in the Act and the way in which damage to endangered species continues to occur, mainly from planning conditions being allowed. Levels of unreasonableness vary, and the word itself is ambiguous. Destroying habitat may or may not be illegal according to the judgment of Planning Authorities, inspectors from the Department of the Environment and the Secretary of State for the Environment. Legislation that overrides the 1981 Act, such as mineral extraction laws, also threatens sites. Officials are often very sympathetic and helpful, recognizing that the protection of endangered species requires a far stronger commitment than presently exists. The Wildlife and Countryside Act has been described by some as a lesson in what happens when you allow too much tinkering with wildlife legislation as it passes through Parliament. Beaten and tatty, the

law is often hard to implement by the worthiest civil servants.

The destruction of the dry lowland heathlands, for example, which still continues, will be a lasting reminder of how a unique habitat of international importance was sliced up in post-war Britain for economic gain. Smooth snakes and sand lizards are still bulldozed and crushed for houses, roads, pipelines and industrial sites. The situation would be farcical if it were not such a national disgrace and embarrassment. Those who have lived and fought for the conservation of dry heathland for the last thirty years or more have lost the war, and are now concerned for the last few battles over remaining scraps of habitat.

'Commoner' reptiles, including marine turtles in British waters, are protected under Schedule 5 of the Wildlife and Countryside Act from sale and killing. However, signs on nature reserves still reinforce the old prejudices against snakes with 'BEWARE ADDERS' often used by lazy gamekeepers and wardens to herd the easily frightened public away from a favourite pheasant or orchid spot. Friendly signs explaining the risk of adder bite in a sensible way are needed.

The Protection of Animals Act 1911 applies to all types of reptiles and could be enforced more frequently. It prevents cruel treatment of reptiles (amongst other animals) which are captive. The criteria for captivity include a situation where an animal is pinioned or prevented from escaping, so a snake being constrained in a small place or pinned by a stick or boot while being killed is being killed illegally. The Dangerous Wild Animals Act 1976 includes many venomous reptiles and the adder is listed. Anyone wishing to hold adders in captivity must follow special guidelines and have a licence and inspections. It is really designed to control the keeping of far more dangerous animals.

Translocations

The word 'translocation' avoids the complications of defining what is an introduction (of a new species) or a re-introduction (of a species previously present) in what is a tricky and sometimes controversial subject. The moving of reptiles away from sites being destroyed for one reason or another has increased the interest in translocations, and there are some claims that the distribution of reptiles in Britain is at least partly due to human translocations over the last few thousand years. It is not hard to picture people carrying snakes and lizards in pots or bags to offshore islands or other isolated places on land.

In 1831 a Mr James Clealand of Ruth Gael House, County Down, Ireland, engaged in an experiment designed to see whether it was the climate that makes Ireland unsuitable for snakes. He bought six grass snakes from Covent Garden market in London and shipped them to Ireland. One might criticize his experimental technique because he rather tactlessly released them fairly close to the tomb of St Patrick. The locals were outraged, a posse was soon formed and most if not all of the snakes were hunted and killed by locals 'in great consternation'.

An introduction of the sand lizards to Doncaster in Yorkshire, earlier this century, resulted in them breeding for a while, but the colony did not survive to spread and they are now absent. A similar experiment on the island of Coll in Scotland has resulted in a few individuals remaining after more than ten years, but numbers are small.

Re-introduction of captive bred and reared sand lizards to their known recent range in Britain have met with better results, including the establishment and recovery of a number of small colonies.

Snakes have also been moved about, but like lizards, the establishing of stable and spreading colonies may take decades. Snakes from sites 'doomed' by development have been used to top-up populations; for example, adders from Frensham Ponds in Surrey were introduced to Epping Forest in 1958, and smooth snakes from Dorset have been used to boost Surrey sites over the last twenty years. The value of such actions is hard to measure. The mixing of populations to some people is considered as genetic pollution and to be avoided wherever possible, while others say that it maintains a flow of genes that is no longer otherwise possible. There can be no doubt, however, that the effect of persecution by humans has reduced many populations way below the maximum number of animals an area can support and that rescue and release in the right places serves as an important short-term conservation activity.

The rules to follow when considering translocations include gaining when possible a good idea of the numbers and distribution of reptiles on the 'donor' and 'receptor' sites. You should consult fully with local naturalists and government scientists, and in many cases their permission may be required. Permission will also be required from the land-owners concerned, and monitoring of the results should be carried out for as long as possible. In short, it is a long and complicated conservation technique to carry out properly. It is certainly no compensation for the loss of an area to development and should hardly ever be considered as such.

The release of non-native snakes and lizards deliberately or by accident includes the snake most commonly imported by dealers, the non-venomous North American Garter snake. It is quite often reported in the wild, though this species has never established a breeding colony, probably due to our cool summer climate. Escaped European species such as wall lizards and green lizards may survive and sometimes form small breeding colonies but these are rarely stable unless protected and enhanced by careful gardening. Green lizards occur on Jersey in the Channel islands, and may have occurred on mainland Britain at some point in the last thousand years. It is difficult to prove this, though an examination for lizard bones in pellets of birds of prey from the last century might yield further clues.

Turtle diary

Just before the Second World War the marine or sea turtles legally became considered as British reptiles, but at that time only considered as the occasional passing migrant. The then Board of Trade undertook to monitor turtle sightings and asked H.M. Coastguards and Receivers of Wrecks to treat marine turtles as 'Royal Fish' under their obligations to act on matters relating to animals belonging to the Crown. As a result of the 1986 review of the 1981 Wildlife and Countryside Act, all marine turtles became fully protected from deliberate capture and killing or injury in UK waters, as it became recognized that some turtles were regular visitors. Until recent years, it was thought that sea turtles were just unlucky individuals caught in Gulf Stream drift in the Atlantic Ocean. This was no doubt true for some of the adult and juvenile turtles washed ashore on the coastlines of Ireland and western England. We now know that leathery or luth turtles are powerful swimmers, well insulated from cold, and that they move northwards in mid-summer to follow concentrations of jellyfish on which they feed. They then move southward as winter approaches. Until quite recently it was suggested that a stranded or captured turtle could be packed in a strong ventilated crate and sent by train to the Natural History Museum in London for identification. Today, stranded or net and line-snarled turtles

The leathery or luth turtle is the most common sea-turtle in British coastal waters.

Many sea-farers know how to carefully release sea turtles from their nets while at sea. Those like this leathery, which are tangled in long-lines, may require further attention as may wounded and exhausted turtles.

must be carefully released following procedures laid down by the Nature Conservancy Council.

Four of the world's seven sea turtles occur in the seas around north-west Europe. In the waters off the British Isles over 330 incidents have been reliably recorded at sea or caught in nets of mackerel and other fishing boats over the last one hundred years or so. The exact fate of the other three species, loggerhead, Kemp's ridley and (rarely) hawksbill which drift into British waters, is less certain. A proportion of beach-stranded turtles have wounds recently inflicted by boat propellers, and this suggests that many more turtles could be around than are reported. The diet of sea turtles includes jellyfish, fish, crustacea, molluscs and sea weeds. Most sea turtles have a hard shell or carapace. This is a hard protective coat, like the bodywork around a car. The surface is made up of a veneer of epidermal shields or 'scutes' which grow to accommodate the growth of the underlying bone. The thick bulk of the shell is formed of hard bone. The shell of the hawksbill turtle is ornate and malleable when heated and is used to make tortoiseshell curios. Its numbers have been greatly depleted in many parts of the world as a result. Leathery or luth turtles rarely exceed two metres in length and 750 kg (1653 lb) but old reports suggest some may reach huge sizes and weights. The other species are considerably smaller. The smooth, leathery skin consists of 1.5 inches of tough greasy cartilage above a thin mosaic-like sheet of small bones. The amount of natural oils in marine

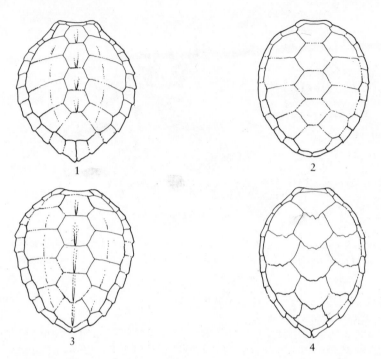

Sea-turtle shells: 1. Kemp's ridley 2. Green 3. Loggerhead 4. Hawksbill.

turtles probably assists with problems from decompression during diving. The leathery turtle may dive as deep as 1,000 metres to feed on jellyfish.

The turtles most frequently stranded on British coastlines are loggerhead turtles, though the occasional Kemp's ridley and hawksbill may also turn up, usually from September until February; younger turtles are more commonly found. The Kemp's ridley is only known to breed in the Gulf of Mexico. Loggerheads may also travel to UK waters from Morocco, where they are known to breed, and the entrance to the Mediterranean where they are frequently seen along the coast of Portugal. Very little is really known about sea turtle movements into British waters. The loggerhead turtle is the one most likely to be encountered by the average holiday-maker on Greek and Turkish beaches, where our desire to holiday has created pressure to build sprawling coastal resorts. These are often on the sandiest spots along the eastern Mediterranean. Turtles must land during the summer to dig a shallow nest, lay eggs and cover them over amongst an obstacle course of buildings, deckchairs and sightseers. The noise and lights from discos,

1st Loggerhead Turtle: 'It wasn't like this when I was a youngster.'
2nd Loggerhead Turtle: 'Looks like we really are in the soup after all.'

hotels and airports at night distract and disorientate both adult and hatchling turtles. By day, the turtles' nests of eggs are crushed by vehicles and the poles of sun-umbrellas. Offshore, during daylight, the turtles are mutilated by speed-boat propellers as they wait just below the surface of the sea for nightfall.

There are very few (if any) records for a fifth species of sea turtle, the green turtle, in British waters, despite its occurrence in the Mediterranean. Green turtles are the most frequently associated with turtles that are eaten, though the eggs of all marine turtles are consumed around the world; rarely, at low sustainable levels. The green turtle is the one from which soup was once a common banquet starter hence its old nick-name 'Mayor's turtle'. Other species of sea turtles can be poisonous. Around 1749 the Bishop of Carlisle is reported to have spoken of a 'green turtle' brought in off Scarborough and sold for a dinner party. The only guest to partake however was taken violently ill soon after.

Information and further reading

There are several books on British reptiles, though few of them remain in print for long. Hunting for them in secondhand and antique book shops is often the only way to find them. Some specialist natural history book services can obtain titles for you. Some of those listed in the references may be found in library collections, while others have been recently updated.

Information on reptiles can be found in technical journals (you may need a good museum, polytechnic or university library and a dictionary of zoological terms). Local conservation groups will often have a reptile contact and local museums and natural history societies are often helpful. You may be able to join in local survey or habitat management efforts. Often the best way to get information is through experience and talking to those who work on reptiles in the field.

Appleby, L.G., *British Snakes* (John Baker (Publishers) Ltd, 1971)

Arnold, E.N., J.A. Burton and D.W.A. Ovenden, *A field guide to the reptiles and amphibians of Britain and Europe* (Collins, London, 1978)

Bell, T., *A History of British Reptiles* (1839)

Buckley, J., *A Guide for the Identification of British Amphibians and Reptiles* (British Herpetological Society, 1980)

Catton, C., and G. James, *The Incredible Heap. A guide to compost gardening* (Pelham Books, London, 1983)

Cooke, A.S., and H.R.A. Scorgie, 'The status of the commoner amphibians and reptiles in Britain, report no. 3, Nature Conservancy Council (1983)

Cooke, M.C., *Our reptiles* (Hardwicke, London, 1865)

Langton, T.E.S., *Protecting Wild Reptiles and Amphibians in Britain* (Report published by the Fauna and Flora Preservation Society, 1986)

Leighton, G.R., *The Life-History of British Serpents and Their Local Distribution in the British Isles* (Blackwood, London, 1901)

Moore, N.W., 'The heaths of Dorset and their conservation', J. Ecol. 50, 369-391 (1962)

Morris, R., and D. Morris, *Men and Snakes* (Sphere Books, London, 1968)

Morrison, N., *The Life-story of the Adder* (Alexander Gordiner, Paisley)

Nature Conservancy Council, *The ecology and conservation of amphibian and reptile species endangered in Britain.* Wildlife Advisory Branch (1983)

Prestt, I., 'An Ecological study of the viper, *Vipera berus,* in southern Britain', J. Zool., London, 164, 373-418 (1971).

Pritchard, P.C.H., *Encyclopedia of Turtles* (TFH Publications, 1979)

Simms, C., *Lives of British Lizards* (Goose and Son, Norwich, 1970)

Smith, M., *The British Amphibians and Reptiles* (Collins New Naturalist Series, 1951)

Stafford, P., *The Adder* (Shire Natural History, 1987)

Steward, J.W., *The Snakes of Europe* (Associated University Press Inc., 1971)

Street, D., *Reptiles of Northern and Central Europe* (Batsford, London, 1979)

Index